# NUTRi BULLET®

## USER GUIDE & RECIPE BOOK

NUTRiBULLET
900 SERIES

To get the **MOST** out of life...
you need to get the **MOST** out of your food!™

## LIFE BOOSTING NUTRIENT EXTRACTION RECIPES

# IMPORTANT SAFEGUARDS AND CAUTIONARY INFORMATION
## SAVE THESE INSTRUCTIONS

### FOR YOUR SAFETY, CAREFULLY READ ALL INSTRUCTIONS BEFORE OPERATING YOUR NUTRIBULLET.

When using electrical appliances, basic safety precautions should always be used, including the following:

- Caution! To avoid risk of electric shock, never immerse the cord, plug, or power base blender in water or other liquids.

- This appliance has a polarized plug (one prong is wider than the other) to reduce the risk of electric shock. This plug will correctly fit in a polarized outlet only one way. If the plug does not fit fully in the outlet, reverse the plug. If it still does not fit, contact a qualified electrician. **Do not modify the plug in any way.**

- The use of attachments not recommended or sold by the manufacturer may cause fire, electric shock, or injury.

- **DO NOT USE THIS PRODUCT WITH ANY TYPE OF ADAPTOR OR VOLTAGE CONVERTER DEVICE. THIS UNIT IS MANUFACTURED IN COMPLIANCE WITH US AND CANADIAN ELECTRICAL STANDARDS AND PLUG TYPES.**
- **USE OF ADAPTERS AND CONVERTERS IS CONSIDERED AN UNAUTHORIZED MODIFICATION OF THE PRODUCT AND AS SUCH VOIDS THE WARRANTY. USE OF THIS PRODUCT IN LOCATIONS WITH DIFFERENT ELECTRICAL SPECIFICATIONS MAY RESULT IN DAMAGE TO THE PRODUCT.**
- **UNPLUG THE NUTRIBULLET WHEN IT IS NOT IN USE. MAKE SURE THE MACHINE IS UNPLUGGED BEFORE ASSEMBLING, DISASSEMBLING, ADDING ADDITIONAL PARTS, AND CLEANING.**

- Do not pull, twist, or mistreat the power cord.
- Do not allow the cord to hang over the side of the counter or table.
- Do not allow cord to touch hot surfaces, including stove.
- Periodically inspect cord and plug for damage. Do not operate any appliance with a damaged cord or plug. If the appliance malfunctions or is dropped or damaged in any manner, discontinue use. Contact Customer Service for assistance in obtaining a replacement.
- Avoid contact with moving parts.
- Keep hands and utensils away from the cutting blade while chopping or blending food to reduce the risk of severe personal injury or damage to the device. A scraper may be used, but only when the blender/food chopper is not running.
- Never allow the motor to run for more than **one minute** at a time, as it can cause permanent damage to the motor. If the motor stops working, **unplug the Power Base and let it cool for an hour** before attempting to use it again. Your **NUTRIBULLET** has an internal thermal breaker that shuts off the unit when it overheats. The Power Base will reset when the unit is unplugged and the thermal breaker cools down.
- To reduce the risk of injury, make sure the blade base is securely screwed onto the cup before placing it on the Power Base and operating the appliance.
- Never leave the **NUTRIBULLET** unattended while it is in use.
- Close supervision is necessary when any appliance is used by or near children.
- Do not use **NUTRIBULLET** outdoors if exposed to inclement weather elements such as rain or other wet conditions.

- Blades are sharp. Handle carefully.
- Check gasket to make sure it is completely seated in the cross blade or flat blade unit before each use.
- The NUTRIBULLET is not intended for use in the microwave. Do not place the NUTRIBULLET Cups, Power Base or accessories in the microwave as this may result in damage to the appliance.
- To reduce the risk of personal injury or damage to the device, keep hands and utensils away from the cutting blade.
- Never blend carbonated beverages. Built-up pressure from released gases can cause container to burst, resulting in possible injury.
- Do not blend the hot liquids in any of the blending vessels.
- Do not run the NutriBullet when the cups are empty.

# WARNING!

- IF YOU ARE TAKING ANY MEDICATION, ESPECIALLY CHOLESTEROL-LOWERING MEDICATION, BLOOD THINNERS, BLOOD PRESSURE DRUGS, TRANQUILIZERS, OR ANTIDEPRESSANTS, PLEASE CHECK WITH YOUR DOCTOR BEFORE CONSUMING ANY OF THE NUTRIBLAST RECIPES.

- THE FOLLOWING LIST OF SEEDS AND PITS CONTAIN CHEMICALS THAT RELEASE CYANIDE INTO THE BODY WHEN INGESTED. DO NOT USE THE FOLLOWING SEEDS AND PITS IN THE NURTIBULLET:
    - APPLE SEEDS
    - APRICOT PITS
    - CHERRY PITS
    - PLUM PITS
    - PEACH PITS

## CLEANING SAFEGUARDS

- RINSE BLADES (AND CUPS) IMMEDIATELY AFTER USE TO PREVENT DEBRIS FROM DRYING AND STICKING TO VESSELS – IF NECESSARY, USE A DISH BRUSH TO LOOSEN ANY DEBRIS.
- HAND WASH ONLY WITH MILD DISH SOAP AND WARM WATER (NOT HOT).
- DRY IMMEDIATELY
- FOR TOUGH DEBRIS, FILL THE CUP ½ FULL WITH WARM (NOT HOT), MILD SOAPY WATER. THEN, SIMPLY TWIST ON THE BLADE, POP IT ON THE BASE AND GIVE IT A RUN FOR 30-45 SECONDS. FOLLOW UP WITH A QUICK BRUSH.
- DO NOT PUT THE BLADES IN THE DISHWASHER. SIMPLY HAND WASH WITH WARM, MILD SOAPY WATER.
- THE NUTRIBULLET CUPS CAN BE WASHED ON THE TOP RACK OF THE DISHWASHER USING THE NORMAL (NOT SANITIZE) CYCLE. THE NUTRIBULLET CUPS AND BLADES SHOULD NOT BE STERILIZED IN BOILING WATER FOR ANY REASON AS THIS WILL WARP THE PLASTIC.
- WHEN WASHING BLADES, DO NOT ATTEMPT TO REMOVE THE GASKET RING. SIMPLY HAND WASH THE BLADES IN WARM, MILD SOAPY WATER. ATTEMPTED REMOVAL OF THE GASKET MAY PERMANENTLY DAMAGE THE BLADE CONFIGURATION AND CAUSE LEAKAGE. IF IN TIME A GASKET BECOMES LOOSE OR DAMAGED, PLEASE CONTACT CUSTOMER SERVICE FOR A REPLACEMENT NUTRIBULLET BLADE HOLDER AT: 1-855-346-8874.

# SAVE THESE INSTRUCTIONS
# FOR HOUSEHOLD USE ONLY

# CLEANING THE NUTRIBULLET

Everyone hates cleaning up, which is just <u>one</u> more reason the NUTRIBULLET is such a wonderful time saver.

**WARNING:**
**ALWAYS UNPLUG THE NUTRIBULLET WHEN CLEANING OR ASSEMBLING.**

## Washing the NUTRIBULLET

Cleaning the **NUTRIBULLET** is so easy… simply place any of the pieces (except for the Power Base and blade holders) on the top shelf of the dishwasher or hand wash with warm soapy water and rinse.

**WARNING:**
**DO NOT WASH THE BLADES IN THE DISHWASHER. THE NUTRIBULLET CUPS CAN BE WASHED IN THE DISHWASHER AND SHOULD BE WASHED ON THE TOP RACK OF THE DISHWASHER USING THE NORMAL (NOT SANITIZE) CYCLE. THE NUTRIBULLET CUPS AND BLADES SHOULD NOT BE STERILIZED IN BOILING WATER FOR ANY REASON AS THIS WILL WARP THE PLASTIC.**

## STUBBORN CLEANUP

If ingredients dry inside the **NUTRIBULLET,** make your cleanup a snap by filling the cup about 2/3 full with warm soapy water and screw on the Milling Blade. Place the cup assembly on the **NUTRIBULLET,** Power Base for about 20-30 seconds. That will loosen the stuck ingredients, and with a light scrub, you'll be all done.

## CLEANING THE NUTRIBULLET POWER BASE

For the most part the Power Base doesn't really get dirty, but if you neglect to twist the blade on to the cup tightly, liquids can leak out and get into the base and activator buttons.

**Here's how to clean it up.**

**Step 1:** The most important thing is to UNPLUG the Power Base!

**Step 2:** Use a damp rag to wipe down the inside and outside of the Power Base.

- **NEVER SUBMERGE THE POWER BASE IN WATER OR PLACE IT IN THE DISHWASHER.**
- Never put your hands or utensils near the moving blade and never use your hands or utensils to press the activator buttons down while the Power Base is plugged in.

# SAVE THESE INSTRUCTIONS
# FOR HOUSEHOLD USE ONLY

# TABLE OF CONTENTS

Introduction . . . . . . . . . . . . . . . . . . . . . . . . . . . . . . . . . . . . . . .9

Am I Healthy? . . . . . . . . . . . . . . . . . . . . . . . . . . . . . . . . . . . . .11

Slowing Down the Aging Process. . . . . . . . . . . . . . . . . . . . . . . . . .13

Are You Eating Your Food. . . . . . . . . . . . . . . . . . . . . . . . . . . . . . .15

The Importance of Eating Nutrient Extracted Food. . . . . . . . . . . . . . .17

The Power of the **NUTRIBULLET** . . . . . . . . . . . . . . . . . . . . . . . . . .19

The Importance of Health and Vitality . . . . . . . . . . . . . . . . . . . . . . 21

The Path to Improved Vitality . . . . . . . . . . . . . . . . . . . . . . . . . . . . 23

    What You Get . . . . . . . . . . . . . . . . . . . . . . . . . . . . . . . . . . . 23

    What Is A **NUTRIBLAST?** . . . . . . . . . . . . . . . . . . . . . . . . . . . . 25

How it Works. . . . . . . . . . . . . . . . . . . . . . . . . . . . . . . . . . . . . . 26

    Extracting . . . . . . . . . . . . . . . . . . . . . . . . . . . . . . . . . . . . . 26

    Milling . . . . . . . . . . . . . . . . . . . . . . . . . . . . . . . . . . . . . . . 27

    Shake Technique. . . . . . . . . . . . . . . . . . . . . . . . . . . . . . . . . 28

    Tap Technique . . . . . . . . . . . . . . . . . . . . . . . . . . . . . . . . . . 29

The Path to Improved Vitality and Longer Life . . . . . . . . . . . . . . . . . .31

    **NUTRIBLAST** . . . . . . . . . . . . . . . . . . . . . . . . . . . . . . . . . . .31

    Eating To Promote Wellness . . . . . . . . . . . . . . . . . . . . . . . . . . 34

Getting Started . . . . . . . . . . . . . . . . . . . . . . . . . . . . . . . . . . . . 37

Seeds to Avoid. . . . . . . . . . . . . . . . . . . . . . . . . . . . . . . . . . . . . 38

How To Build A **NUTRIBLAST** . . . . . . . . . . . . . . . . . . . . . . . . . . . 39

**NUTRIBLAST** Recipe Ideas . . . . . . . . . . . . . . . . . . . . . . . . . . . . .41

    Phase 1. . . . . . . . . . . . . . . . . . . . . . . . . . . . . . . . . . . . . . .42

    Phase 2. . . . . . . . . . . . . . . . . . . . . . . . . . . . . . . . . . . . . . 43

Phase 3. . . . . . . . . . . . . . . . . . . . . . . . . . . . . . . . . . . . . . . . . 46

**NUTRIBLAST** For Life . . . . . . . . . . . . . . . . . . . . . . . . . . . . . . . . .51

Eat Sensibly All Day Long . . . . . . . . . . . . . . . . . . . . . . . . . . . . . 53

**THE SUPERFOOD 6-WEEK TRANSFORMATION PLAN!**. . . . . . . . . . . . 54

The "Five to Thrive" Keys to Success . . . . . . . . . . . . . . . . . . . . . 57

Tips and Tricks for A Successful Program . . . . . . . . . . . . . . . . . . 62

The Program. . . . . . . . . . . . . . . . . . . . . . . . . . . . . . . . . . . . . . 68

Stage 1 Meal Plan. . . . . . . . . . . . . . . . . . . . . . . . . . . . . . . . . .70

Stage 2 Meal Plan. . . . . . . . . . . . . . . . . . . . . . . . . . . . . . . . . . 72

Stage 3 Meal Plan. . . . . . . . . . . . . . . . . . . . . . . . . . . . . . . . . .74

Stage 1 **NUTRIBLASTS**. . . . . . . . . . . . . . . . . . . . . . . . . . . . . .76

Stage 2 **NUTRIBLASTS**. . . . . . . . . . . . . . . . . . . . . . . . . . . . . . 77

Stage 3 **NUTRIBLASTS**. . . . . . . . . . . . . . . . . . . . . . . . . . . . . . 79

On Track Snacks. . . . . . . . . . . . . . . . . . . . . . . . . . . . . . . . . . .81

Super Soups . . . . . . . . . . . . . . . . . . . . . . . . . . . . . . . . . . . . . 86

Wellness Wraps and Sandwiches . . . . . . . . . . . . . . . . . . . . . . . 91

Good Grains Side Dishes. . . . . . . . . . . . . . . . . . . . . . . . . . . . . 95

(Mostly) Rawlicious Side Salads . . . . . . . . . . . . . . . . . . . . . . . .102

Dinners. . . . . . . . . . . . . . . . . . . . . . . . . . . . . . . . . . . . . . . . .108

Stage 1 Journal. . . . . . . . . . . . . . . . . . . . . . . . . . . . . . . . . . .117

Stage 2 Journal. . . . . . . . . . . . . . . . . . . . . . . . . . . . . . . . . . .131

Stage 3 Journal. . . . . . . . . . . . . . . . . . . . . . . . . . . . . . . . . . .145

# WHY ARE WE SO SICK?

Heart Disease kills
## 7.1 million
people worldwide per year

in 2009,
## 7.9 million
deaths were due to
CANCER

by 2030,
cancer will claim
## 11 million
lives per year

in 2030
## 336 million
people worldwide will be diabetic

2/3 of Americans over the age of 20 are
## OBESE

# CONGRATULATIONS ON YOUR NEW LEASE ON LIFE

Congratulations on your purchase of the **NUTRIBULLET**—the world's first Nutrition Extractor! We are thrilled that you have chosen the path to optimum health and vitality!

By the time you finish reading this paragraph, four Americans will have had a heart attack and another four will have had a stroke or heart failure. Heart attack is the leading killer in developed countries. Worldwide, cancer kills 7.6 million people annually. Deaths from cancer are projected to reach over 11 million in 2030!

Throughout the world 171 million people have been diagnosed with diabetes and over 500 million people are clinically obese. As per the World Health Organization, obesity is a leading preventable cause of death worldwide and authorities view it as one of the most serious public health problems of the 21st century.

**What is going on? Why are we so sick?** The vast majority of these diseases and conditions can be <u>directly</u> attributed to consumption of the "western diet," which consists of too many processed foods that are high in sugar and salt and too few fruits and vegetables.

It seems that we have forgotten what we learned in grade school science class, that we are **made up of cells and that cells need only 3 simple things to survive – food, water and air.** We have a big say in whether our cells are healthy or unhealthy. We make that choice every time we put something in our mouths. If we choose to eat processed fat and sugar-laden meals, we choose to seriously increase our risk of cancer, diabetes, and heart disease.

Fortunately, YOU, as a **NUTRIBULLET** owner, have chosen to treat your body to the highest possible level of nutrition – nutrient-extracted food! You have chosen to THRIVE and FEEL GREAT. Congratulations on making such a powerful decision. With the **NUTRIBULLET,** it's as **easy as possible** to get on—and stay on—the path to optimum health.

***NOTE:*** *The information contained in our guide and recipe book is not a substitute for regular health care. Always consult your physician regarding health and nutrition.*

# AM I HEALTHY?

The best way to gauge your current and future health is to ask yourself, "How am I feeling right now?" Do I feel great? Do I have lots of energy? Do I feel attractive? Pain Free? Ready to take on the world?

Or do I feel fat? Tired? Miserable? Sick? Or just, blah?

It's time to look at yourself and ask: Is my food making me stronger and more resistant to debilitating disease? Or is it making me weaker, making it harder for my body to do what it needs to stay healthy?

**WE ARE WHAT WE EAT!** Who are you going to be tomorrow? How about when you are 40? 60? 80?

## How do I feel today?

_____

_____

_____

_____

_____

## New Goals:

_____

_____

_____

_____

Date: ___/___/_____

*The NUTRIBULLET is not like any blender you have at home! It's a Nutrition Extractor.*

# SLOWING DOWN
# THE AGING PROCESS

Every cell in our body has a lifespan and when it dies, it gets replaced with a new cell. Over the course of the next 7 years every cell in our body will be regenerated. This fascinating cell replacement process is very intricate and yet a bit imperfect. The new cells often contain small errors and THIS is why we age. The aging process becomes accelerated by the amount of free radicals we take in on a daily basis. Things like smoking, drinking alcohol and eating unhealthy foods speed up the aging process and put us on a fast track to developing disease. Being healthy, and most importantly, feeding ourselves healthy food, slows down the aging process so we can enjoy every day to the fullest.

The **NUTRIBULLET** makes it so easy and so delicious to feed every one of our cells healthy, wholesome, easily absorbed superfoods to achieve optimal health. The power of the **NUTRIBULLET** squeezes every last drop of disease-fighting anti-oxidants, joint-relieving Omega 3s, and muscle-strengthening protein from the foods we eat and drink every day.

**To get the most out of life, you need to get the most out of your food!**

# What would you rather eat?

## 1/8 cup

nutrient extracted
flax seed in a **NUTRIBLAST**

**or**

**or**

## 60

cups of brocolli

## 100

slices of whole wheat bread

# ARE YOU EATING YOUR FOOD?

Think about eating a bunch of red grapes. You pull a handful off the stems, rinse them off, pop one in your mouth, and spit out the seeds. If you were juicing these same grapes, the juicer would catch the skins and seeds in the strainer basket. But did you know over 100 research studies on grapes have shown that the highest levels of nutrients reside primarily in the stem, skin and seeds of the grapes rather than in the juicy middle section?

That's right! Most of those health benefits we hope to gain come from a category of disease-fighting antioxidants called polyphenols. Flavinoids, phenolic acids, and resveratrol—the most beneficial polyphenols in grapes— are most concentrated in the parts we discard. It's time to stop throwing this vital disease-reversing nutrition in the trash! The **NUTRIBULLET** enables its users to access super nutrients that would otherwise go to waste.

It's like this: to consume the same amount of cancer-blocking enzymes found inside 1/8 cup of extracted flax seed, we would need to eat roughly 60 cups of fresh broccoli or 100 slices of whole wheat bread. Or, we could add 1/8 cups of flax seeds and some berries into a **NUTRIBLAST,** and enjoy a delicious Flax Berry Smoothie in just seconds!

www.nutribullet.com

# THE IMPORTANCE OF EATING NUTRIENT EXTRACTED FOOD

In our busy world, we often don't take the time to eat healthfully or properly chew what we eat. These tendencies make extra work for our digestive system as it attempts to extract nutrients from poorly chewed and nutritionally void food. Over time, this stress reduces the strength of digestive enzymes. These depleted enzymes, coupled with the weakened stomach acids that come with age, result in a digestive system that cannot break foods down enough to access and utilize the vital nutrition inside. When our body fails to absorb these nutrients day after day, week after week, we become weaker and weaker and more vulnerable to sickness and chronic disease.

Supplements may offer some relief to this issue of nutrient deficiency, but our bodies are not designed to process nutrients delivered by non-food sources. While they may be useful to a certain extent, supplements are by no means a substitution for proper nutrition because the human body is designed to acquire nutrients from whole, unprocessed foods.

Even when we eat healthfully, our digestive system has a hard time accessing all of the vitamins, minerals and phytonutrients found in the foods we eat. The most reliable way to ensure our bodies get the nourishment they need is through **NUTRITION EXTRACTION.** When fruits, vegetables, seeds, and nuts are broken down to their most digestible form before they are consumed, the digestive system can easily absorb the best they have to offer. Fortunately, the **NUTRIBULLET** does just that!

***NOTE:*** *The information contained in our guide and recipe book is not a substitute for regular health care. Always consult your physician regarding health and nutrition.*

www.nutribullet.com

# THE POWER THE NUTRIBULLET

The **NUTRIBULLET** is not like any other blender on the market. Its 900-watt motor, all-new Extractor Blade, and Magic Bullet-exclusive Cyclonic Action breaks the pulp, skin, seeds, and stems of the plants we eat down into tiny drinkable particles, unlocking the full scope of nutrients contained within them. Chewing, juicing, or blending with ordinary blenders can't rival the **NUTRIBULLET's NUTRITION EXTRACTING** power.

With **NUTRITION EXTRACTION,** the gold mine of zinc and magnesium inside watermelon seeds, the wealth of Omega-3 fatty acids and healthy enzymes in blackberry seeds, and the powerful anti-oxidants in broccoli stems become bioavailable—ready for optimal absorption into the bloodstream! Get ready to experience the rush that true, healthful living supplies!

# THE IMPORTANCE OF HEALTH AND VITALITY

## Add Healthy Years to Your Life

"If we eat wrongly, no doctor can cure us. If we eat rightly, no doctor is needed." – Victor G. Rocine

Eating an abundance of nutrient-extracted food can add years to your life. Not just any years, but healthy, vibrant, disease-free years. **Who doesn't want to live a long, happy life?** By embracing a healthy lifestyle and fueling your body with the vital nutrition it deserves, you can expect to see the following changes:

- Balanced internal pH
- Beautiful hair, skin, and nails
- Decreased risk of chronic disease
- Enhanced mood
- Increased energy
- Increased athletic performance
- Improved digestion (decreased constipation, gas, bloating, and IBS)
- Improved sleep
- Lower cholesterol
- Lower blood pressure
- Relieved diabetes and pre-diabetic conditions
- Weight loss
- Younger looking, glowing skin with visibly decreased wrinkles and improved elasticity

1 High-torque Power Base

2 Tall Cups with 1 Handled Lip Ring
and one Regular Lip Ring

New! Flip-Top To-Go Lid
with Oversized Cup

1 Short Cup

Bonus Life Changing
Recipes Book

# THE PATH TO IMPROVED VITALITY!

## What You Get:

### The NUTRIBULLET comes with 15 pieces

2 Extractor Blades

2 Stay-fresh Resealable Lids

1 User Manual / Recipe Book

1 Pocket Nutritionist

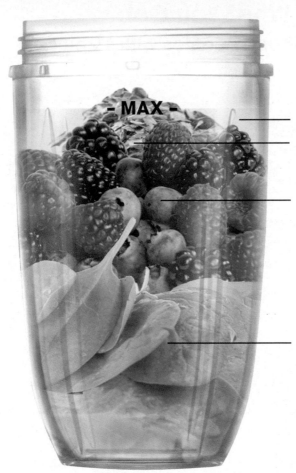

- MAX -

Add water to MAX line

Add "boost"

50% fruit
(as many varieties
as possible!)

50% leafy greens
(2 cups = 1 serving)

## NUTRIBLAST

# THE PATH TO IMPROVED VITALITY!

## What Is A NUTRIBLAST?

The **NUTRIBLAST** is a nutrient-extracted drink designed to feed your system as many servings of easily absorbable fruits and vegetables as possible. All variations follow a very simple basic formula: **50% leafy greens, 50% fruit, and ¼ cup of seeds, nuts, or "super boosts." Add enough water to cover ingredients, twist on the blade, and blend.**

The **NUTRIBLAST** makes an ideal breakfast beverage, but you can enjoy extracted nutrition any time of the day! You will be amazed by how energetic and healthy you feel from enjoying this satisfying raw **NUTRITION-EXTRACTED** goodness every day!

Start with one **NUTRIBLAST** a day (see recipe suggestions on page 42). As you begin to feel the amazing rewards that accompany a diet rich in **NUTRITION EXTRACTED** foods, feel free to enjoy **TWO NUTRIBLASTS** a day. Boundless energy, restful sleep, mental clarity, and the overall feeling of well being that comes from true nourishment await! The more you blast, the better you'll feel!

# HOW IT WORKS

## Extracting

**1** Fill ingredients into the Tall or Oversized Cup.

**2** Twist the Extractor Blade onto the Tall Cup and tighten by hand to make sure the vessel is sealed.

**3** Press the vessel blade side-down onto the Power Base and extract for no longer than 1 minute. If more extraction is needed, wait 1 minute, then repeat the extraction process in 1 minute intervals up to 3 times as needed to achieve the desired consistency. If more than 3 1-minute extractions are needed, allow the power base to cool for 2-3 minutes after the third extraction before beginning the next round.

# Shake Technique

Sometimes, if you over fill the cups with ingredients or don't put enough water, the results can increase the density of the mixture. This makes it hard for the ingredients toward the top of the cup to make it down to the blade. If some of your ingredients are having a hard time making it down to the blade, simply use the Shake technique.

**1** Remove the cup and blade assembly from the Power Base.

**2** With the cup and blade assembly in hand, shake it like a cocktail shaker. Then put it back on the Power Base.

# HOW IT WORKS

## Tap Technique

For really stubborn ingredients that are clinging to the side of the cup instead of being recirculated into the cutting zone, simply use the Tap technique.

**1** Take the cup and blade assembly off the Power Base and Tap the cup and blade assembly on the counter to force the ingredients down into the blades.

**2** Place the cup and blade assembly onto the Power Base and finish processing.

# THE PATH TO IMPROVED VITALITY AND LONGER LIFE!

## NUTRIBLASTS: MAKE IN A SNAP

It only takes seconds to make these nutritional masterpieces! **NUTRIBLASTS** taste great, they're fun to make, and easy to clean up!

### Replace Heavy Meals!

Most people feel satisfied with one **NUTRIBLAST** for breakfast, but feel free to have a healthy snack later in the morning if you get hungry. A whole grain granola bar, hardboiled egg, or yogurt should tide you over until lunch. See our **SUPERFOOD 6-WEEK TRANSFORMATION PLAN** on page 54 for great meal and snack ideas and new ways to incorporate **NUTRIBLAST's** into your life!

### Feel the Difference!

Adding five to ten servings of raw, nutrition-extracted fruits and vegetables to your day will have an AMAZING effect on how you look and feel. **First,** you will notice a **burst of energy** you won't believe you had in you! Second, you will attain a feeling of overall **wellness**—fewer aches and pains, deeper sleep, a stronger immune system, and more even mood and energy levels. This process can occur very quickly, and **you will continue to feel better and better** as you continue to enjoy nutrition-extracted foods.

### See the Difference!

Within a few days, you will begin to see the difference – a little extra room in the waistline of your pants, a glow to your skin, shiny hair, a sparkle in your eye. **People will start to comment on how good you look.** Enjoy the compliments – you deserve them! Who knew it would be SO easy to feel and look this much better? Keep up the great progress!

# THE PATH TO IMPROVED VITALITY AND LONGER LIFE!

## Nothing Feels as Good as Feeling Good

As you get further into your daily **NUTRIBLAST** program, your skin will improve and you'll wake up feeling well rested. You may lose a few pounds, and you may even lower your blood pressure and cholesterol levels. Yet no matter what changes arise, you will doubtlessly feel so much better than you do at this moment. This isn't a diet program you'll suffer through, but a lifestyle choice you'll want to stick to. You'll feel so good adding **NUTRITION-EXTRACTED** food into your diet that you won't want to stop! The more you add, the better you'll feel, and nothing feels as good as feeling good!

## Add Years to Your LIFE

By eating this wonderfully nutritious, **NUTRITION-EXTRACTED** food, you very well could be adding years to your life by preventing and even reversing the chronic diseases that plague so many of us – including heart disease, cancer, diabetes, and immune disorders.

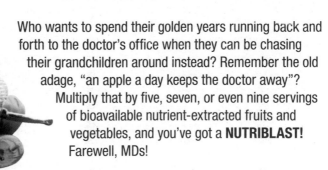

Who wants to spend their golden years running back and forth to the doctor's office when they can be chasing their grandchildren around instead? Remember the old adage, "an apple a day keeps the doctor away"? Multiply that by five, seven, or even nine servings of bioavailable nutrient-extracted fruits and vegetables, and you've got a **NUTRIBLAST!** Farewell, MDs!

# Eating To Promote Wellness

| FOOD TYPE | ENJOY | AVOID |
|---|---|---|
| Dairy | Non-fat cottage cheese, unsweetened yogurt, goat's milk, raw or skim buttermilk, non-dairy almond milk. | Soft cheese, all pasteurized or artificially colored cheeses and ice cream. |
| Eggs | Boiled or poached (no more than 4 a week). | Fried or pickled eggs. |
| Fish | All broiled or baked freshwater white fish, salmon or canned tuna in water. | Fried fish, shell fish, salted fish and all fish canned in oil. |
| Fruits | All unsweetened fresh, frozen or dried fruits. | Canned, bottled, or frozen fruits with sweeteners added. |
| Grains | All whole grains and products containing 100% whole grains. | All white flour products, white rice, white pasta, crackers, cereal and instant cereals or oatmeal. |
| Meats | Skinless turkey, chicken or lamb. | Beef, pork, hot dogs, luncheon meat, all processed meat, duck, goose and organ meat. |
| Nuts | All fresh, raw nuts (peanuts no more than once a week). | All salted, roasted nuts and peanuts if history of allergy. |
| Oils (fats) | All cold-pressed oils including corn, safflower, sesame, olive, flaxseed, soybean, sunflower and canola, margarine made from cold pressed oil and eggless mayonnaise. | All saturated fats, hydrogenated margarine, refined processed oils, shortening and hardening oils. |

# THE PATH TO IMPROVED VITALITY AND LONGER LIFE!

## A Wonderful Side Benefit

After incorporating **NUTRIBLASTS** into you daily routine, you will find your cravings for sweet, salty, and fatty junk food significantly reduced. Once your body realizes how great nutrient-extracted food makes you feel, you will actually begin craving HEALTHY foods. FANTASTIC—roll with it! We've included a chart titled "EATING TO PROMOTE HEALTH AND WELLNESS" as well as a sample menu to help you eat for optimum health and vitality outside of the **NUTRIBULLET** system.

## Eating To Promote Wellness

| FOOD TYPE | ENJOY | AVOID |
|---|---|---|
| Seasonings | Garlic, onions, all herbs, apple cider vinegar, tamari, miso, seaweed and dulse. | Black pepper, white pepper, salt and all types of vinegar (except pure apple cider vinegar). |
| Soups | Homemade soups: lentil, bean, pea, veggie, barley, brown rice, onion. Low salt organic soups. | Canned soups made with salt, preservatives, stock or MSG. |
| Sprouts and Seeds | All slightly cooked sprouts and all raw seeds. | All seeds cooked in oil or salt. |
| Sweets | Small amounts of raw honey, pure maple syrup, stevia and blackstrap molasses. | White, brown or cane sugar. Corn syrup, sugared candies. |
| Vegetables | All raw, fresh, frozen (no salt or additives). | All canned or frozen with salt or additives. |

**NOTE:** *The information contained in our guide and recipe book is not a substitute for regular health care. Always consult your physician regarding health and nutrition.*

**Give all pieces (except Power Base) a quick rinse with soapy water before using!**

Getting started couldn't be easier! Get your **NUTRIBULLET** unit out and give the cups and blades a quick rinse with warm soapy water. Then get ready to create your first **NUTRIBLAST!**

## Now it's time make your first
# NUTRIBLAST!

# GETTING STARTED

## STEP 1: ADD 50% LEAFY GREENS TO THE TALL CUP.

Two cups makes up a full serving of leafy greens, so that's the amount you want to work up to in the first few weeks. That's about two good-sized handfuls.

## STEP 2: ADD 50% FRUIT TO THE TALL CUP.

A serving of fruit is generally a cup. We suggest adding a banana or 1/2 of an avocado to every 'Blast for the "creamy" factor. Then add three more fruits (or more if you can fit it!) to your **Tall Cup.**

## STEP 3: ADD WATER TO TASTE. We suggest you

add water to the MAX LINE. If you like a thicker 'Blast, add less water. If you like a thinner 'Blast, add more water, but never beyond the MAX LINE.

## STEP 4: ADD YOUR BOOST (optional). Add a

handful of nuts, seeds or goji berries to pack in some essential fatty acids! Boosts make for a more nutritious and filling **NUTRIBLAST**.

## STEP 5: TWIST ON THE NUTRIBULLET

BLADE, EXTRACT, ENJOY! Twist on the blade, then place the cup on the **Power Base.** Push down and twist until it locks into the "on" position (you'll know because it will be running!). Keep extracting until you achieve a very smooth consistency. Twist on the handle and bottoms up!

Add water to MAX line

Add "boost"

50% fruit
(as many varieties
as possible!)

50% leafy greens
(2 cups = 1 serving)

- MAX -

## NUTRIBLAST

# WARNING

**BAD SEEDS:** While **NUTRITION EXTRACTION** can be amazingly beneficial, not all fruit seeds and rinds are created equal. The following seeds and pits contain a chemical that releases <u>cyanide</u> into the body when ingested. DO NOT USE the following seeds and pits in the NUTRIBULLET:
- Apple Seeds
- Apricot Pits
- Cherry Pits
- Plum Pits
- Peach Pits

# HOW TO BUILD A NUTRIBLAST

## Enjoy a 2-Day!

### 4 Easy Steps!
1. Fill the cup with 50% leafy greens + 50% fruit.
2. Fill only up to the **MAX** line with water (add ice if you want).
3. Add 1/8 to 1/4 nuts and/or seeds, if desired.
4. Twist on the **NUTRIBULLET** blade and blend until smooth.

---

### LEAFY GREENS – 50%
Choose one from the following list of leafy greens or, mix and match! Fill the **Tall Cup** up to 50% with leafy greens. Work up to 2 full cups (2 handfuls) of leafy greens per Blast.

- ○ Collard Greens
- ○ Kale
- ○ Romaine
- ○ Spinach
- ○ Spring Greens
- ○ Swiss Chard

---

### FRUITS – 50%
Choose as many fruits as you want to equal 50% of your **NUTRIBLAST.**

- ○ Apple
- ○ Avocado
- ○ Banana
- ○ Blackberry
- ○ Blueberry
- ○ Cantaloupe
- ○ Cranberry
- ○ Fig
- ○ Green Grapes
- ○ Guava
- ○ Honeydew
- ○ Kiwi
- ○ Mango
- ○ Nectarine
- ○ Orange
- ○ Papaya
- ○ Peach
- ○ Pear
- ○ Pineapple
- ○ Plum
- ○ Raspberries
- ○ Red Grapes
- ○ Strawberry
- ○ Watermelon

---

### BOOSTS - 1/4 CUP
The following ingredients are an important part of your **NUTRIBULLET NUTRIBLAST,** adding additional fiber and nutrition to every sip. Add 1/8 to ¼ cup to any Blast.

**Nuts**
- ○ Almonds
- ○ Cashews
- ○ Walnuts

**Seeds**
- ○ Chia Seeds
- ○ Flax Seeds
- ○ Hemp Seeds
- ○ Pumpkin Seeds
- ○ Sesame Seeds
- ○ Sunflower Seeds

**Super Chargers**
- ○ Goji Berries
- ○ Acai Berries

# NUTRIBLAST RECIPE IDEAS!

If you've been slight on your fruit and vegetable consumption, it's best to start off a bit slow. Add a good handful of leafy greens and match that same amount with fruit. Start with one **NUTRIBLAST** a day. You may have a bit of a gassy stomach for the first few days as your body gets used to having so much fiber. Don't worry, this will pass (no pun intended)!

If you are looking to achieve the BEST POSSIBLE RESULTS, start with a **NUTRIBLAST** for breakfast, then squeeze in another later in the day. **NUTRIBLASTS** also make a wonderful dessert. Satisfy that sweet tooth with vital nutrition!

**Please note:** If you are taking any medication, especially cholesterol-lowering medication, blood thinners, blood pressure drugs, tranquilizers, or antidepressants, **please check with your doctor before consuming any of the NUTRIBLAST recipes.**

## WARNING!

- IF YOU ARE TAKING ANY MEDICATION, ESPECIALLY CHOLESTEROL-LOWERING MEDICATION, BLOOD THINNERS, BLOOD PRESSURE DRUGS, TRANQUILIZERS, OR ANTIDEPRESSANTS, PLEASE CHECK WITH YOUR DOCTOR BEFORE CONSUMING ANY OF THE NUTRIBLAST RECIPES.
- THIS PROGRAM IS NOT INTENDED TO REPLACE MEDICAL ADVICE OR BE A SUBSTITUTE FOR A PHYSICIAN. IF YOU ARE SICK OR SUSPECT YOU ARE SICK, YOU SHOULD SEE A PHYSICIAN. IF YOU ARE TAKING A PRESCRIPTION MEDICATION YOU SHOULD NEVER CHANGE YOUR DIET WITHOUT FIRST CONSULTING YOUR PHYSICIAN BECAUSE ANY DIETARY CHANGE MAY AFFECT THE METABOLISM OF THAT PRESCRIPTION DRUG.

As you're getting started with your **NUTRIBLASTS,** we suggest using greens with a mild taste like spinach or spring greens. The fruits you use will easily mask their flavor, making for a tasty, refreshing drink. Experiment with water quantities to find your ideal consistency. The more water you use, the thinner your **NUTRIBLAST,** and vice versa. Remember to never go beyond the MAX LINE. Fight any temptation you have to add processed ingredients like fruit juice. Whole, unprocessed foods will give you the best results.

These Phase One recipes are perfect for first time **NUTRIBLASTERS,** but don't be afraid to get creative. Use the guide on page 39 to concoct your own masterpieces. You can even share your favorites with us on Facebook! "Like" us at facebook.com/thenutribullet and join our wonderful community!

## Toxin Cleansing Blast

Flush toxins from your body with this delicious, fruity concoction.

- 1-2 handfuls of rinsed spinach
- 1 cored pear
- 1 banana
- 1 cored apple
- 1 cup of pineapple
- water

## Vita-Berry Blast

Ward off cancer, heart disease, and viruses with this sweet and tasty blast of flavonoids!

- 1-2 handfuls of rinsed spinach
- 1 cup of blueberries
- 1 banana
- 1 handful strawberries
- water

## The Immune Booster

Keep healthy even during flu season with this delicious elixir packed with antioxidant goodness.

- 1-2 handfuls of rinsed spring greens
- 1 banana
- 1 peeled orange
- 1 cup of pineapple
- 1 handful of blueberries
- water

**NOTE: Because the size of all fruits and vegetables vary, please use the max line on the cups as your guide. Do not fill beyond the max line.**

# NUTRIBLAST RECIPE IDEAS!

## Morning Glory
Start your day with boundless energy with this flavorful blend.
- 1-2 handfuls spinach
- 1 avocado
- 1 cup strawberries
- 1 cup mango
- 1/4 cup goji berries
- water

## Nutty Nectar
Go nuts with this vitamin rich blast of flavor.
- 1-2 handfuls spinach
- 1 banana
- I cup strawberries
- 1 cup honeydew
- 1/8 cup walnuts
- water

## Tropical Tonic
Boost your immune system with this vitamin C rich drink.
- 2 handfuls spring greens
- 1 avocado
- juice of ½ lemon
- 1 cup mango
- 1 cup papaya
- 1/4 cup pumpkin seeds
- water

## Protein Powerhouse
Packed full of protein, this super satisfying blend keeps you energized for hours.
- 2 handfuls spring greens
- 1 avocado
- 1 cup raspberries
- 1 orange
- 1 cup mango
- 1/8 cup cashews
- water

## Peachy Pick-me-up
Healthy fats and flavor abound in this tasty treat.
- 2 handfuls spring greens
- 1 banana
- 1 peach
- 1 cup honeydew
- 1 cup blackberries
- water

**NOTE: Because the size of all fruits and vegetables vary, please use the max line on the cups as your guide. Do not fill beyond the max line.**

**STAGE 2**

Now that you are well on your way to becoming a **NUTRITION EXTRACTION** expert, it's time to mix up those greens and get some new vitamins and minerals down the hatch! As you progress, try not to fall into an ingredient rut. The more you vary the greens, fruits, vegetables, and boosts you add into your **NUTRIBLASTS,** the more nutritional benefits you will receive.

Some of the Phase Two greens have a more distinct flavor than their Phase One counterparts. You may want to balance the 'green' flavor of ingredients like romaine and butter lettuce with sweeter fruits and boosts. Almonds, cashews, and walnuts balance flavors nicely and add filling protein to your beverage. Keep experimenting, and be sure to post your favorites on our Facebook page!

At this point, it's a great idea to add a second **NUTRIBLAST** to your daily routine. **NUTRIBLASTS** make a wonderful afternoon snack or dessert after a light dinner. The more extracted nutrition you include in your diet, the better you are going to feel. Enjoy better sleep, boundless energy, and decreased aches and pains. Here's to a second daily **NUTRIBLAST!**

## Energy Elixir

Add some serious pep to your step with this delicious, energizing elixir. A perfect afternoon pick me up.
- 2 handfuls of rinsed spring greens
- 1 banana
- 1 cup red grapes
- 1 cored pear
- 1/8 cup of walnuts
- water

## Fountain of Youth

Look and feel years younger by enjoying this age-reversing blend.
- 2 handfuls of rinsed spinach
- 1 cup of red grapes
- 1 banana
- 1 cup of strawberry
- 1/8 cup of almonds
- 1 tsp maca powder
- water

**NOTE: Because the size of all fruits and vegetables vary, please use the max line on the cups as your guide. Do not fill beyond the max line.**

# NUTRIBLAST RECIPE IDEAS!

## Longevity Elixir

Feel the years disappear with this light and snappy blend.

- 2 handfuls romaine
- 1 avocado
- 1 cucumber
- 1 cup cantaloupe
- 1/4 cup cashews
- 1 mint leaf
- water

## Nature's Candy

Balance hormones by way of this fantastic tasting treat.

- 2 cups butterhead lettuce
- 1 cored pear
- 1 cored apple
- 1 cup blueberries
- 1 banana
- 1 tsp maca powder
- water

## Get Up and Goji

Power up with this antioxidant-rich flavor extravaganza.

- 2 cups butterhead lettuce
- 1 cup honeydew
- 1 cup cantaloupe
- 1 cup watermelon
- 1 banana
- 1/8 cup goji berries
- water

## Antioxidant Fusion

Fight off free radicals and add years with this tasty blast.

- 2 handfuls of butterhead lettuce
- 1 banana
- 1 orange
- 1 cup pineapple
- 1 cup mango
- 1/4 cup almonds
- water

**NOTE: Because the size of all fruits and vegetables vary, please use the max line on the cups as your guide. Do not fill beyond the max line.**

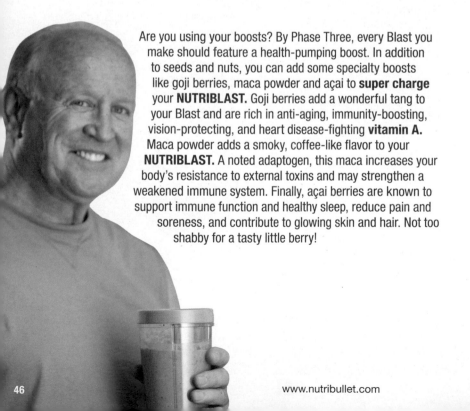

**STAGE 3**

How are you feeing, **NUTRIBLAST** master? Join us on Facebook (www.facebook.com/nutribullet) and share all your wonderful stories! We can't wait to hear about (and try) your favorite **NUTRIBLASTS!**

Congratulations. You've made it to Phase Three! Ready for some hardcore greens? Of course you are!

As we say in the **NUTRIBLAST** world, "the more bitter, the better!" Bitter greens like kale and Swiss chard contain amazing amounts of **calcium** and **magnesium**—minerals that support healthy bones. Additionally, dark, bitter greens are full of cancer-fighting antioxidants **beta carotene, vitamin E,** and **manganese.** Considered liver chi stimulants in Chinese medicine, these greens also serve as great detoxifiers.

Are you using your boosts? By Phase Three, every Blast you make should feature a health-pumping boost. In addition to seeds and nuts, you can add some specialty boosts like goji berries, maca powder and açai to **super charge** your **NUTRIBLAST.** Goji berries add a wonderful tang to your Blast and are rich in anti-aging, immunity-boosting, vision-protecting, and heart disease-fighting **vitamin A.** Maca powder adds a smoky, coffee-like flavor to your **NUTRIBLAST.** A noted adaptogen, this maca increases your body's resistance to external toxins and may strengthen a weakened immune system. Finally, açai berries are known to support immune function and healthy sleep, reduce pain and soreness, and contribute to glowing skin and hair. Not too shabby for a tasty little berry!

# NUTRIBLAST RECIPE IDEAS!

## Life Boost Blast

Start your day with a blast of calcium and magnesium.
No supplement ever tasted this good!

- 1-2 handfuls of rinsed kale
- 1 pitted peach
- 1 banana
- 1 handful of strawberries
- 1/8 cup flax seeds
- 1/8 cup of goji berries
- water

## Digestive Health Elixir

Rich with enzymes, this pineapple blend helps to
get your digestive system running smoothly.

- 1-2 handfuls of rinsed swiss chard
- 1 banana
- 1 cup of cored pineapple
- 1 apple
- 1 cup of blueberries
- ¼ cup of soaked goji berries
- water

## Liver and Colon Tonic

Detox away with this tasty treat.

- 1-2 handfuls of rinsed collard greens
- 1 banana
- 1 cup of pineapple
- 1 cup of red grapes
- ¼ cup of hemp seeds
- water

**NOTE: Because the size of all fruits and vegetables vary, please use the max line on the cups as your guide. Do not fill beyond the max line.**

# Banana Berry Vitality Blend

Grab a quick energy boost with our Banana Berry Blend!
- 2 handfuls kale
- 1 banana
- 2 figs
- 1 cored apple
- 1 handful blueberries
- $1/8$ cup walnuts
- $1/4$ cup acai berries
- water

# Kaleacado Blast

Unleash your libido with a luscious Kaleacado Blast!
- 2 handfuls kale
- 1 avocado
- 1 cup watermelon
- red grapes
- 1 tsp maca powder
- ¼ cup strawberries
- water

# Melon Blast

Maximize your fiber and melt away pounds with a mouthwatering Melon Blast!

- 2 handfuls kale
- 1 banana
- 1 cup green grapes
- 1 cup cantaloupe
- 1 handful strawberries
- $1/8$ cup cashews
- water

**NOTE: Because the size of all fruits and vegetables vary, please use the max line on the cups as your guide. Do not fill beyond the max line.**

# NUTRIBLAST RECIPE IDEAS!

## Power Booster
Pick up your pace with a delicious, nutritious Power Booster.
- 2 handfuls Swiss chard
- 1 banana
- 1 nectarine
- 1 cup blueberries
- ¼ cup goji berries
- water

## Swiss Mix
Mix it up with this flavor-packed, nutrient-rich blend.
- 2 handfuls Swiss chard
- 1 banana
- 1 plum
- 1 cup green grapes
- ⅛ cup pumpkin seeds
- water

## Free Radical Fighter
Give free radicals a knock-out punch with a tasty Free Radical Fighter!
- 2 handfuls Swiss chard
- 1 avocado
- 1 cup watermelon
- 1 cup blackberries
- 1 fig
- ½ cup blueberries
- ⅛ cup flax seeds
- water

**NOTE: Because the size of all fruits and vegetables vary, please use the max line on the cups as your guide. Do not fill beyond the max line.**

# NUTRIBLAST FOR LIFE

Take it to the limit! You are surely feeling the incredible benefits of nutrient-extracted foods. Get as many fruits and greens in your drink as you can! Down that tall cup and have a second **NUTRIBLAST** as an evening snack. Add those boosts! The more goodness you ingest, the better you'll feel!

**NOTE:** *The information contained in our guide and recipe book is not a substitute for regular health care. Always consult your physician regarding health and nutrition.*

# EAT SENSIBLY ALL DAY LONG

To get the greatest health benefits from your **NUTRIBLAST,** we encourage you to eat sensibly throughout the entire day. This will become easier and easier as your body grows accustomed to the surge of nutrients your daily (or twice-daily) **BLAST** provides. You will find that your body will lose its cravings for salty, fatty, and sugary foods in favor of the good stuff! Check page 34 for suggestions of healthy foods that support the **NUTRIBLAST** lifestyle, turn to page 54 to embark on the **NUTRIBULLET SUPERFOOD 6-WEEK TRANSFORMATION PLAN.**

We know you will enjoy your **NUTRIBULLET** and all the benefits it provides. Cheers to you for choosing optimum health!

For those looking to seriously transform their health and their lives, look no further than this **THE SUPERFOOD 6-WEEK TRANSFORMATION PLAN!**

The next 60 pages are FULL of the meal plans, eating schedules, recipes, tips and tricks you need to overhaul your health and regain lost vitality.

Those who have followed this plan have increased their energy, lost weight, and improved the way they look and feel all in just weeks!! Are you ready to do the same?

Turn the page to find out more!

# WARNING!

- IF YOU ARE TAKING ANY MEDICATION, ESPECIALLY CHOLESTEROL-LOWERING MEDICATION, BLOOD THINNERS, BLOOD PRESSURE DRUGS, TRANQUILIZERS, OR ANTIDEPRESSANTS, PLEASE CHECK WITH YOUR DOCTOR BEFORE CONSUMING ANY OF THE NUTRIBLAST RECIPES.
- THIS PROGRAM IS NOT INTENDED TO REPLACE MEDICAL ADVICE OR BE A SUBSTITUTE FOR A PHYSICIAN. IF YOU ARE SICK OR SUSPECT YOU ARE SICK, YOU SHOULD SEE A PHYSICIAN. IF YOU ARE TAKING A PRESCRIPTION MEDICATION YOU SHOULD NEVER CHANGE YOUR DIET WITHOUT FIRST CONSULTING YOUR PHYSICIAN BECAUSE ANY DIETARY CHANGE MAY AFFECT THE METABOLISM OF THAT PRESCRIPTION DRUG.

*NOTE:* *The information contained in our guide and recipe book is not a substitute for regular health care. Always consult your physician regarding health and nutrition.*

# THE NUTRIBULLET SUPERFOOD 6-WEEK TRANSFORMATION PLAN
## Because Nothing Feels as Good as Feeling Good

In the next six weeks, you are going to dramatically improve the way you look and feel by doing one simple thing—adding **NUTRITION EXTRACTED** whole foods to your daily diet! Our easy-to-follow **6-WEEK TRANSFORMATION PLAN** gives you all the tools you need to revitalize your body. Separated into three 2-week long phases, the program gradually introduces more and more fresh, raw produce and wholesome ingredients to your lifestyle.

Each phase of this program rests firmly on the foundation of the **NUTRIBLAST**—the ultra-nutritious, tasty shake that is easy to make and even easier to drink! Chock full of fruit, greens, and goodness, **NUTRIBLASTS** only take seconds to make and blast your body with optimal nutrition. As you progress in the Program, you will increase the number and nutritional density of the **NUTRIBLASTS** you drink.

The ease and portability of **NUTRIBLASTS** make the **SUPERFOOD 6-WEEK TRANSFORMATION PLAN SO EASY TO FOLLOW.** You'll be enjoying these nutritious "super meals" a few times a day without cooking or dirtying pots and pans. Clean up is a snap, and you won't believe how easy it is to take your **NUTRIBLAST** on the go! Work at an office? Work outside? No problem. Just twist on the To-Go lid and your life boosting super meal is ready for the road!

Worried that **NUTRIBLASTS** won't fill you up? Fear not! You will NEVER go hungry on the **SUPERFOOD 6-WEEK TRANSFORMATION PLAN** because in addition to **NUTRIBLASTS,** you ALSO get to enjoy delicious snacks, savory soups, zesty salads and **hearty dinners.** Simply follow the following Five to Thrive Keys to Success and soon you will truly learn that "nothing feels as good as feeling good!"

# THE "FIVE TO THRIVE" KEYS TO SUCCESS

**1** **EXTRACT Your Nutrients!**

**2** **Eat WHOLE Foods!**

**3** **COMBINE Your Foods Properly**

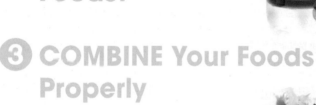

**4** **Eat HALF RAW at All Meals**

**5** **Indulge INTELLIGENTLY**

# THE "FIVE TO THRIVE" KEYS TO SUCCESS

To get the **MOST** out of life, you need to get the **MOST** out of your food. The following 5 steps will get you on the fast track to optimum health throughout the three phases of your **6-WEEK LIFEBOOST PROGRAM:**

## ❶ Extract Your Nutrients!

We are what we eat? Not Entirely. We are what we absorb, and our bodies often fail to absorb the essential nutrients they need.

In our busy lives, we rarely take the time eat healthfully, and very few of us chew foods the way doctors recommend. Because of these habits, our bodies have a harder and harder time digesting and absorbing what we eat. Depleted, overworked digestive enzymes coupled with the weakened stomach acids that come with age cannot break food down to the point where we can access and utilize the nutrition inside. In other words, we don't absorb most of the nutrition contained in our food.

In fact, statistics say that we absorb 10% fewer nutrients every ten years we age. By the time we reach the age of 50, we are only absorbing 50% of the foods (nutrients) we eat. And each year that passes we absorb less and less.

When our body is denied this essential nutrition day after day, week after week, we lose our vitality and become more vulnerable to sickness and chronic disease.

**Fortunately, the NUTRIBULLET breaks down food to its most absorbable state, so it is essentially/basically "pre-digested."** This process is known as **NUTRITION EXTRACTION.** When you consume this nutrition-extracted food, studies show that your body absorbs 90% of the nutrients it contains! This is how the **NUTRIBULLET** turns ordinary food into super food!

www.nutribullet.com

# ➋ Eat Whole Foods!

Food, according to Webster's Dictionary, is any substance that enables one to live and grow—anything that nourishes. Based on this definition, hardly anything in the Standard American Diet can be considered food!

The Standard American Diet is largely made up of processed foods. These food-like substances contain added ingredients, such as salt, sugar, high fructose corn syrup, chemically altered preservatives, and trans fats that serve no nutritional purpose in the body. In fact, many of these ingredients can actually destroy the body and ruin our health! All convenience foods are processed, so if you didn't make it yourself, chances are you can't eat it during this program.

Whole foods, on the other hand, are unprocessed foods. They do not contain ingredients that you cannot pronounce or substances your grandparents wouldn't recognize. They do not come in a box or squeezable tube or microwaveable tray. They are not artificially seasoned or covered in unhealthy sauce.

Whole foods are foods in their original form. They are whole grains, fruits, vegetables, beans, legumes, and meats. Whole foods contain huge amounts of antioxidant vitamins, minerals, and phytochemicals that protect your body from free radicals and disease.

These are the foods we will eat for the next 6 weeks.

Sound intimidating? Have no fear. Our **SUPERFOOD 6-WEEK TRANSFORMATION PLAN** recipes are quick and easy to make, not to mention delicious! We are confident that you'll be thrilled with the fabulous recipes included in this program. Stick with our menu for six weeks and you will see first hand how eating the **SUPERFOODS** improves your mood, energy, and life!

# THE "FIVE TO THRIVE" KEYS TO SUCCESS

## ③ Combine Your Foods Properly

Most of us have been brought up with the idea that a wholesome meal contains one serving of protein, one of starch and one or two servings of vegetables. However, studies show that separate digestive enzymes break down proteins and carbohydrates, and when these enzymes enter your gut at the same time, they cancel out each other's effectiveness. This slows down your digestive process, leaving you tired, sluggish, bloated, gassy and uncomfortable. Who needs that?

**So, never eat protein and starch together. Enjoy meals composed of starches and veggies or proteins and veggies.** To make it simple, our plan suggests starch and salad for lunch and protein and salad for dinner. Pair salad vegetables with whole grain starches or starchy vegetables during the day, and eat salad vegetables with lean protein at night. You will notice a difference in how your body feels and performs!

Here is a list of **LIFEBOOST** friendly starches, salad vegetables (low-starch vegetables), and lean proteins to guide you through your program:

| SALAD VEGETABLES LOW STARCH | STARCHES | LEAN PROTEINS |
| --- | --- | --- |
| All leafy greens, artichoke, asparagus, sprouts, broccoli, brussels sprouts, cabbage, carrots, cauliflower, celery, cucumber, eggplant, jicama, leeks, mushrooms, onions, peppers, radishes, summer squash, tomato, zucchini | **Whole Grains:** whole wheat, brown rice, barley, quinoa, oats, wheat berry, bulgur wheat, popcorn, millet<br><br>**Starchy Vegetables:** beets, potatoes, sweet potatoes, yams, corn, beans, butternut squash, acorn squash, parsnips, peas | **Poultry:** chicken breast, turkey breast<br><br>**Seafood:** salmon, tilapia, halibut<br><br>**Red Meat:** Lean beef including round roast/tip, sirloin, and lean ground |

www.nutribullet.com

# ❹ Eat Half Raw at All Meals

At least half of each meal you consume during your transformation plan should consist of raw fruit or vegetables, and this is why:

When foreign substances enter the body, the immune system sends white blood cells through the blood stream to "attack" these invaders. As a result, body parts become inflamed as white blood cells attempt to defend their precious tissues. While this reaction serves to protect the body, chronic (continued over time) inflammation is one of the leading causes of health decline, and plays a key role in the development conditions like Alzheimer's, arthritis, cancer, heart attack, lupus, psoriasis, and stroke—to name just a handful.

Two different studies in 2005 researched the effect eating a mostly raw vegetarian diet had on the body. The first, published in the Archive of Internal Medicine, found that subjects who ate a raw vegetarian diet showed significantly less inflammation in their bodies than the control group, who ate the Standard American Diet of cooked meat, processed carbohydrates, and salty fats. The second, published in the Journal of Nutrition found that those who followed a mostly raw food diet significantly lowered their LDL Cholesterol—the kind that is stored in your artery walls, causing the inflammation that leads to heart disease.

The **SUPERFOOD 6-WEEK TRANSFORMATION PLAN** recommends that all meals consist of at least 50% raw vegetables to fight the stress, strain , and unnecessary risks of excess inflammation. What a relief on your entire body!

# ❺ Indulge intelligently

On the seventh day, God said "Let there be chocolate!" At the end of every week, reward yourself with the divine taste of antioxidant-packed dark chocolate. Choose any of the following treats from the list to your right as a healthy indulgence.

And there was chocolate and antioxidants. And it was good.

## DARK CHOCOLATE

**Suggestions:**
Green and Black's Organic Dark – 85% Cacao, Dagoba Eclipse – 87% Cacao, Scharffen Berger Extra Dark – 82% Cacao, Valrhona Noir Extra Amer – 85% Cacao, Sacred Chocolate – All

# TIPS AND TRICKS FOR A SUCCESSFUL PROGRAM

1 Be prepared

2 Move past mistakes

3 Be (somewhat) flexible

4 Drink Water, Naturally Flavored Water, and Herbal Teas

5 Write it down

6 Clean Cupboards, Clean Body

7 Snack Attack

8 Don't Shop Hungry

9 Eat before a party or dinner

**NOTE:** *The information contained in our guide and recipe book is not a substitute for regular health care. Always consult your physician regarding health and nutrition.*

We understand that embarking on any lifestyle change can seem daunting, but with the **SUPERFOOD 6-WEEK TRANSFORMATION PLAN,** you are going to look and feel so good that any changes you make are WELL worth the effort! And NOTHING—not even cake or cookies—feels as good as feeling good!

We are confident that you will find that the more you follow this plan, the more you will WANT to follow this plan and continue on your quest to optimal health.

However, temptation is always a reality, and our fast paced lifestyles often pose a challenge to our healthy eating goals. The following tips and tricks will help your plan go as smoothly as possible.

# ❶ Be prepared

A well-laid path is easiest to follow. Most of this program requires homemade meals and snacks. The more of these dishes you have on hand during the week, the easier and more efficient it will be for you to follow the plan. When it's snacktime or lunchtime and you already know EXACTLY what you will be eating, you are far less likely to be tempted by something that doesn't fit into your program. It's a great idea to spend a weekend morning planning out your meals and snacks for the week; then purchase and prepare everything ahead of time. Freeze any dishes you plan on eating during the week; if you work outside of your home, bring your **TRANSFORMATION** meals on the road with you. **Half a day of preparation will set you up for a week of excellent eating.** Plus, you won't believe the time and money you'll save making your own foods!

# TIPS AND TRICKS FOR A SUCCESSFUL PROGRAM

## ❷ Move past mistakes

Despite our best efforts, we humans are not perfect. If you accidentally munch a cupcake at your daughter's birthday party or eat a bag of chips as an emergency snack, don't give up on your plan. Forgive yourself and continue with the program as if those processed pieces never entered your system.

## ❸ Be (somewhat) flexible

On the same note as above, do not deny your body any of its needs. This plan is specially formulated to meet and exceed daily nutrition requirements, but everybody and every body is different. If you find yourself famished or overly full, adjust your plan accordingly. Just be sure your body, not your head, is driving the adjustment and make sure that any extra portions fit with the plan's guidelines outlined in the "**FIVE TO THRIVE" KEYS TO SUCCESS.**

## ❹ Drink Water, Naturally Flavored Water, and Herbal Teas

While you will be drinking many of your meals in **NUTRIBLAST** form on this plan, it's very important not to forget to **drink plenty of water.** Staying hydrated will not only remind your stomach that you are satisfied, but also keep you focused, energetic, and less likely to stray from your goals. If you prefer flavored beverages, infuse your $H_2O$ with mint, cucumber, lemon, or lime. Enjoy herbal and decaf green teas as much as you like.

If you are a coffee drinker, limit yourself to one cup a day. Replace milk and cream with almond or hemp milk, and sugar with stevia extract.

Hold off on Happy Hour as best you can during your **SUPERFOOD 6-WEEK TRANSFORMATION PLAN.** Alcohol bogs down your digestive system and will hinder your transformation. A glass of wine here or there is ok, but for optimum results, ditch the booze for a spell.

## ⑤ Write it down

While the **NUTRIBULLET** provides the framework for this plan, it's up to you to fill in the specifics of what you consume. Keep track of meal and snack choices as well as portion sizes in the journal portion of this book. Record your meal and snack times as well to get a sense of your body's hunger cycle.

## ⑥ Clean Cupboards, Clean Body

Remove temptation by clearing your cupboards of processed, Standard American Diet foods. **Keep only clean, whole foods in your house.** Your body will thank you.

## ⑦ Snack Attack

It happens to the best of us. One minute we're waxing holistic about our new clean lifestyle, and the next we're clawing through our pantries to find something, ANYTHING, sweet/salty/crunchy/all of the above (this is when **Tip #6** is on your side).

Fear not. There are plenty of **SUPERFOOD 6-WEEK TRANSFORMATION PLAN**-approved snacks that fit these criteria. When hunger strikes, turn to the following suggestions. Just be sure to cap your cravings at ONE SERVING.

| Salty/Crunchy | Sweet |
| --- | --- |
| • Mary's Gone Crackers<br><br>• Two Moms in the Raw Crackers<br><br>• Edamame (1/2 c in shell with a sprinkle of salt)<br><br>• Oil-free popcorn: Place ½ cup of popcorn in a large (3qts or bigger) microwave-safe glass bowl, cover and heat on high for 4-5 minutes. Stay nearby and remove as soon as popping slows down to prevent burning. | • Frozen banana "ice cream": Freeze one banana unpeeled, in chunks. When a craving hits, blend the fruit in the NutriBullet short cup with a tsp of water or unsweetened almond/hemp milk until smooth. Add in walnuts and cacao nibs after blending for a special treat. It's amazing how similar the texture and flavor is to real banana ice cream—you'll wonder why you didn't switch to this version long ago!<br><br>• Milk Shake: mix unsweetened almond milk, raw cacao powder, 6 to 7 cashews, a pinch of stevia, and goji berries with ice in the Short Cup. Pulse until mixture reaches an even milkshake consistency.<br><br>• Raw vegan chocolate chip cookies:<br>  – 2/3 c pitted dates<br>  – 1/4 c cashews, almonds, or walnuts<br>  – 1/4 c raw cacao nibs, chocolate chips, or 70% cacao bittersweet chocolate chips<br>  – 1/4 tsp pure vanilla extract<br>  Extract dates, nuts, and vanilla in the short cup until they reach a dough-like consistency. Mix in chocolate chips and form into bars, balls, or other shapes.<br><br>• 1/2 oz raw cacao nibs with 1 Tbsp raisins |

## Sweet (continued)

- Power of Cacao: **NUTRIBLAST**
  - 1.5 cups of coconut water
  - 2 Tbsp honey
  - 45 blueberries (about 1 cup)
  - 15 raspberries
  - 3 Tbsp raw cacao nibs
  - 2 Tbsp raw almonds.

Place all ingredients in the **NUTRIBULLET** and extract.

# ⑧ Don't Shop Hungry

Shopping while hungry will make you more tempted to purchase highly processed and overpriced convenience foods. Grocery shop after you've had a meal or snack, and remember that the fewer ingredients that "form" a food, the better that food is for your body!

# ⑨ Eat before a party or dinner

While on the plan, you may find that social functions and restaurants do not serve foods that meet your requirements. Eat a **TRANSFORMATION** meal before heading to a dinner party, restaurant gathering, or any other social event. Order a green salad or snack on raw veggies during the gathering, and stay focused on the company you're with, not the cuisine.

# THE PROGRAM

Get ready to feel the best you have in years! Try not to approach this adventure in health as a strict 6-week commitment. You don't have to, because within a few days of following the plan, you will feel so good that you will be thrilled to eat this way, and nothing feels as good as feeling good!

## NUTRIBLAST

A **NUTRIBLAST** is made up of 50% greens and 50% fruit. During your **SUPERFOOD 6-WEEK TRANSFORMATION PLAN,** we provide recipes as suggestions but you can always create your own blend by combining what you have in the fridge.

— MAX LINE —

———————— Add water to MAX LINE
———————— Add "boost"

———————— 50% fruit (as many varieties as possible!)

———————— 50% leafy greens (2 cups = 1 serving)

# NUTRIBLAST

## LEAFY GREENS - 50%

Choose one from the following list of leafy greens or, mix and match! Fill the **Tall Cup** up to 50% with leafy greens. Work up to 2 full cups (2 handfuls) of leafy greens per Blast.

- ◯ Collard Greens
- ◯ Kale
- ◯ Romaine
- ◯ Spinach
- ◯ Spring Greens
- ◯ Swiss Chard

## FRUITS - 50%

Choose as many fruits as you want to equal 50% of your **NUTRIBLAST.**

- ◯ Apple
- ◯ Avocado
- ◯ Banana
- ◯ Blackberry
- ◯ Blueberry
- ◯ Cantaloupe
- ◯ Cranberry
- ◯ Fig
- ◯ Green Grapes
- ◯ Guava
- ◯ Honeydew
- ◯ Kiwi
- ◯ Mango
- ◯ Nectarine
- ◯ Orange
- ◯ Papaya
- ◯ Peach
- ◯ Pear
- ◯ Pineapple
- ◯ Plum
- ◯ Raspberries
- ◯ Red Grapes
- ◯ Strawberry
- ◯ Watermelon

## BOOSTS - 1/4 CUP

The following ingredients are an important part of your **NUTRIBULLET NUTRIBLAST,** adding additional fiber and nutrition to every sip. Add 1/8 to ¼ cup to any Blast.

**Nuts**
- ◯ Almonds
- ◯ Cashews
- ◯ Walnuts

**Seeds**
- ◯ Chia Seeds
- ◯ Flax Seeds
- ◯ Hemp Seeds
- ◯ Pumpkin Seeds
- ◯ Sesame Seeds
- ◯ Sunflower Seeds

**Super Chargers**
- ◯ Goji Berries
- ◯ Acai Berries

***NOTE:*** *The information contained in our guide and recipe book is not a substitute for regular health care. Always consult your physician regarding health and nutrition.*

# STAGE ①

**Stage 1** takes place during **week 1** and **week 2** of your program. During this period, you will:

- Enjoy a Stage 1 **NUTRIBLAST** for your daily breakfast
- Cut your animal product (meat, cheese, dairy) intake to 1 serving per day
- Cut your cooking oil intake to 1 Tbsp of olive oil/day

## MEAL PLAN

### ① BREAKFAST:

Choose any Stage 1 **NUTRIBLAST** recipe on page 76, or create your own using any combination of fruits, greens, and boosts listed on page 69.

### ② MORNING SNACK:

Choose any Snack from the On-Track Snack List on page 81.

### ③ LUNCH:

Choose one dish from category A and one dish from category B.

| A: | B: |
|---|---|
| • 1.5 cups Super Soup (pg 86) | • 2 cups Rawlicious Side Dish (pg 102) |
| • 1.5 cups Good Grains (pg 95) | • 2 cups Salad Greens of your choice |
| • 1 Wellness Wrap/ Sandwich (pg 91) | • 2 cups mixed raw veggies of your choice |

## MEAL PLAN

**4** **AFTERNOON SNACK:**

Choose any snack from the On-Track Snack List on page 81.

**5** **DINNER:**

Choose one main dish from either category A or B and a side dish from category C.

| A: | or | B: | with | C: |
|---|---|---|---|---|
| **(4 oz Protein)** | | • 1.5 cups Vibrant Veggie Dinner of your choice (pg 109) | | **(2 cups of)** |
| • **Poultry:** chicken breast, turkey breast | | | | • Rawlicious Side Salad (pg 102) |
| • **Seafood:** salmon, halibut, tilapia, trout | | | | • Salad Greens of your choice |
| • **Red Meat:** Lean beef including round roast/tip, sirloin, and lean ground | | | | • Mixed raw veggies of your choice |

**6** **DESSERT:**

While we don't recommend daily desserts for the program, we do understand that everyone needs the occasional sweet treat. At the end of each week, enjoy one chocolate bar from our list on page 61. If you find you are desperate for treats during the week, check out our sweet section on page 66. Remember, this plan is for YOU and your health, so you are the best judge when it comes to indulging.

# STAGE ❷

Stage 2 takes place during **week 3** and **week 4** of your program. During this period, you will:

- Enjoy a stage 2 **NUTRIBLAST** for your daily breakfast
- Include a small Green **NUTRIBLAST** as part of your daily lunch
- cut your animal product intake to 4 to 6 servings/week
- cut your cooking oil intake to 1 Tbsp of olive oil or coconut oil per day

## MEAL PLAN

### ❶ BREAKFAST:

Choose any Stage 2 **NUTRIBLAST** recipe on page 77, or create your own using any combination of fruits, greens, and boosts listed on page 69.

### ❷ MORNING SNACK:

Choose any Snack from the On-Track Snack List on page 81.

### ❸ LUNCH:

Enjoy one green **NUTRIBLAST** recipe on page 78 (Column A) with any dish from column B. Column C is optional.

| A: | with | B: | or | C: |
|---|---|---|---|---|
| Short Cup **NUTRIBLAST** Recipes on (pg 78)  | | • 1.5 cups Super Soup (pg 86)<br><br>• 1.5 cups Good Grains (pg 95)<br><br>• 1 Wellness Wrap/ Sandwich (pg 91) | | **(2 cups of)**<br>• Rawlicious Side Dish (pg 102)<br><br>• Salad Greens of your choice<br><br>• Mixed raw veggies of your choice |

## MEAL PLAN

### ④ AFTERNOON SNACK:

Choose any snack from the On-Track Snack List on page 81.

### ⑤ DINNER:

Choose one main dish from either category A or B and a side dish from category C.

| A: | or | B: | with | C: |
|---|---|---|---|---|
| **(4 oz Protein)** | | • 1.5 cups Vibrant Veggie Dinner of your choice (pg 109) | | **(2 cups of)** |
| • **Poultry:** chicken breast, turkey breast | | | | • Rawlicious Side Salad (pg 102) |
| • **Seafood:** salmon, halibut, tilapia, trout | | | | • Salad Greens of your choice |
| • **Red Meat:** Lean beef including round roast/tip, sirloin, and lean ground | | | | • Mixed raw veggies of your choice |

### ⑥ DESSERT:

While we don't recommend daily desserts for the program, we do understand that everyone needs the occasional sweet treat. At the end of each week, enjoy one chocolate bar from our list on page 61. If you find you are desperate for treats during the week, check out our sweet section on page 66. Remember, this plan is for YOU and your health, so you are the best judge when it comes to indulging.

# STAGE ❸

**Stage 3** takes place during the **week 5** and **week 6** of your program. During this period, you will:
- Enjoy a stage three **NUTRIBLAST** for your daily breakfast
- Enjoy a large green **NUTRIBLAST** with lunch
- Eat fewer servings of animal products (meat, cheese, dairy), 6 or fewer servings per 10-day perior
- Cut your cooking oil intake to 1/2 Tbsp of olive oil or coconut oil per day

## MEAL PLAN

**❶ BREAKFAST:**

Choose any Blast recipe from the Stage 3 **NUTRIBLAST** menu on page 79, or create your own using any combination of fruits, greens, and boosts listed on page 69.

**❷ MORNING SNACK:**

Choose any Snack from the On-Track Snack List on page 81.

**❸ LUNCH:**

Pair one large green **NUTRIBLAST** (pg 78) with one dish from category B.

| A: | or | B: |
|---|---|---|
| Short Cup **NUTRIBLAST** Recipes on (pg 78)  | | • 1.5 cups Super Soup (pg 86)<br><br>• 1.5 cups Good Grains (pg 95)<br><br>• 1 Wellness Wrap/ Sandwich (pg 91) |

## MEAL PLAN

**4** ## AFTERNOON SNACK:

Choose any snack from the On-Track Snack List on page 81.

**5** ## DINNER:

Choose one main dish from either category A or B and a side dish from category C.

| A: | or | B: | with | C: |
|---|---|---|---|---|
| **(4 oz Protein)** | | • 1.5 cups Vibrant Veggie Dinner of your choice (pg 109) | | **(2 cups of)** |
| • **Poultry:** chicken breast, turkey breast | | | | • Rawlicious Side Salad (pg 102) |
| • **Seafood:** salmon, halibut, tilapia, trout | | | | • Salad Greens of your choice |
| • **Red Meat:** Lean beef including round roast/tip, sirloin, and lean ground | | | | • Mixed raw veggies of your choice |

**6** ## DESSERT:

While we don't recommend daily desserts for the program, we do understand that everyone needs the occasional sweet treat. At the end of each week, enjoy one chocolate bar from our list on page 61. If you find you are desperate for treats during the week, check out our sweet section on page 66. Remember, this plan is for YOU and your health, so you are the best judge when it comes to indulging.

## I. Immunity Mix
- 50% Spinach
- 50 % mixture of fruit:
  - 1 whole orange with rind
  - 1/2 of lemon with rind
  - 1/2 lime with rind
  - 1" chunk of ginger
  - Sprinkle of sea salt
  - 2 Tbsp organic raw honey

(Top with water to MAX LINE & extract)

## II. Vita-Berry Blast
- 50% Spinach
- 50 % mixture of fruit:
  - 1/2 cup blueberries
  - 1 cup strawberries
  - 1 banana

(Top with water to MAX LINE & extract)

## III. Protein Powerhouse
- 50% Spring Greens
- 50 % mixture of fruit:
  - 1/2 avocado
  - 1 cup raspberries
  - 1/2 cup mango
  - 10 cashews

(Top with water to MAX LINE & extract)

## IV. Morning Glory
- 50% Spinach
- 50 % mixture of fruit:
  - 1/2 avocado
  - 1/2 cup mango
  - 1 Tbsp goji berries

(Top with water to MAX LINE & extract)

## VI. Inflammation Elimination
- 50% Spring Greens
- 50 % mixture of fruit:
  - 1/4 lime with rind
  - 1/4 lemon with rind
  - 1/4 grapefruit with rind
  - 1 Tbsp flax seeds
  - 1/2 tsp tumeric

(Top with water to MAX LINE & extract)

## OR Mix and Match
**the following ingredients for your personalized blast:**

### Greens
Fill 50 % of your cup with:
- Spring Greens
- Spinach

### Fruit
Mix and match the following to fill 50% of your cup:
- cup of pineapple, mango, honeydew, blackberries, strawberries, or raspberries
- apple
- avocado
- banana
- orange
- peach
- pear

### Boosts
Top off your cup with the following amounts of these ingredients:
- 10 walnut halves
- 10 cashews
- 1 Tbsp goji berries
- 1/4 cup pumpkin seeds
- 1/4 cup hemp seeds

# STAGE ❷ NUTRIBLASTS

## I. Hormone Balancer (male)
- 50% Spring Greens
- 50 % mixture of fruit:
  - 1/4 small beet
  - 10 red seedless grapes
  - 2 small broccoli florets
  - 15 blueberries
  - 1/2 handful of pumpkin seeds
  - 1-2 Tbsp olive oil

(Top with water to MAX LINE & extract)

## II. Hormone Balancer (female)
- 50% Butterhead Lettuce
- 50 % mixture of fruit:
  - 1/2 pitted peach
  - 1/2 cup blueberries
  - 3 Brazil nuts
  - 1 tsp maca powder

(Top with water to MAX LINE & extract)

## III. Longevity Elixer
- 50% Romaine
- 50 % mixture of fruit:
  - 1/2 avocado
  - 1 cucumber
  - 1 cup cantaloupe
  - 12 cashews
  - 1 mint leaf

(Top with water to MAX LINE & extract)

## IV. Fountain of Youth
- 50% Spinach
- 50 % mixture of fruit:
  - 1/2 cup red grapes with seeds
  - 1/2 cup raspberries
  - 10 almonds
  - 1 tsp maca powder

(Top with water to MAX LINE & extract)

## V. Antioxidant Fusion
- 50% Butterhead Lettuce
- 50 % mixture of fruit:
  - 1/2 banana
  - 1/2 orange
  - 1/2 c pineapple
  - 10 almonds
  - 1 Tbsp cacao powder

(Top with water to MAX LINE & extract)

## OR Mix and Match
the following ingredients for your personalized blast:

### Greens
Fill 50 % of your cup with:
- Spring Greens
- Spinach

### Fruit
Mix and match the following to fill 50% of your cup:
- blackberries, strawberries, or raspberries
- pineapple, mango, honeydew, or cantaloupe
- apple
- avocado
- banana
- orange
- peach, pitted
- pear
- cup of red grapes (with seeds)

### Required Boosts
(at least one these)
Top off your cup with the following amounts of these ingredients:
- 10 walnut halves
- 10 almonds
- 12 cashews

### Other Boosts
Top off your cup with the following amounts of these ingredients:
- 1 tsp maca powder
- 1 Tbsp sesame seeds
- 1 Tbsp chia seeds

# STAGE ② GREEN DRINKS

☺ = Good for beginners!

Add one small green drink to your Stage 2 lunch. You can replace your raw salad with this drink, or you can enjoy both.

## I. Jumping Ginger
- 1/2 carrot or 5 baby carrots
- 1 handful of parsley
- 1 lemon, peeled
- 1/2 apple, cored and seeded
- 1-inch piece of ginger root
- 1/2 avocado

(Top with water to MAX LINE & extract)

## ☺ II. Banana Kale Bonanza
- 50% kale (about 5 leaves)
- 1/2 cup frozen mixed berries
- 1 banana
- 1 Tbsp hulled hemp seed

(Top with water to MAX LINE & extract)

## ☺ III. Avocado Watercress
- 1-inch piece gingerroot
- 1 handful watercress
- 1 stalk celery
- 1 handful of spinach
- 1/2 pear
- 1/2 avocado
- 1 banana
- 1/2 cup frozen mixed berries

(Top with water to MAX LINE & extract)

## ☺ IV. Green Fever
- 50% spinach
- 1 banana
- 1 tomato

(Top with water to MAX LINE & extract)

## V. Tomavocado
- 50% mixed greens
- 1/2 avocado
- 1 tomato
- 1 handful of cilantro
- juice of 1/2 lime

(Top with water to MAX LINE & extract)

## ☺ VI. Mango Kale
- 50% kale
- 50% frozen mango

(Top with water to MAX LINE & extract)

## OR Mix and Match the following ingredients for your personalized blast:

### Greens
Fill 50 % of your cup with one or more of the following:
- Spring Greens
- Spinach
- Kale
- Parsley
- Cilantro
- Watercress

### Fruits and Vegetables
Mix and match the following to fill 50% of your cup:
- blackberries, strawberries, or raspberries
- mango
- apple
- avocado
- banana
- lemon or lime
- pear
- carrot
- stalk of celery
- tomato
- cucumber
- bell pepper

### Other
Add these ingredients for a pop of flavor and health benefits:
- 1-inch piece of gingerroot
- 1 Tbsp hemp seed
- pinch (1/2 tsp) chili powder

# STAGE ❸ NUTRIBLASTS

Stage 3 **NUTRIBLASTS** introduce some serious greens. The health benefits of these greens are so great, we hope you can handle the taste. Our saying is "the bitterer, the better," but if you can't enjoy these Stage 3 drinks as is, replace a portion of your greens with a milder green like spring greens or spinach. However, these dark greens are so good for you, do your best to include them!

## I. Life Booster
- 50% Rinsed Kale
- 50 % mixture of fruit:
  - 1/2 pitted peach
  - 1/2 c strawberries
  - 1/2 avocado
  - 10 walnut halves
  - 1 Tbsp chia seeds
  - 1 Tbsp goji berries

(Top with water to MAX LINE & extract)

## II. Banana Berry Vitality Blend
- 50% Rinsed Kale
- 50 % mixture of fruit:
  - 1/2 banana
  - 1/2 cup blueberries
  - 10 walnut halves
  - 1 tsp maca powder

(Top with water to MAX LINE & extract)

## III. Power Booster
- 50% Swiss Chard
- 50 % mixture of fruit:
  - 1/2 banana
  - 1/2 pitted nectarine
  - 10 almonds
  - 1 Tbsp raw cacao powder

(Top with water to MAX LINE & extract)

## IV. Digestive Health Elixir
- 50% Rinsed Swiss chard
- 50 % mixture of fruit:
  - 1/2 cup pineapple
  - 1/2 cup strawberries
  - 3 Brazil nuts
  - 1 Tbsp raw cacao powder

(Top with water to MAX LINE & extract)

## V. Kaleacado Blast
- 50% Kale
- 50 % mixture of fruit:
  - 1/2 avocado
  - 1/2 cup watermelon
  - 1/2 cup blueberries
  - 12 cashews

(Top with water to MAX LINE & extract)

## VI. Melon Blast
- 50% Kale
- 50 % mixture of fruit:
  - 1/2 cup raspberries
  - 1/2 cup cantaloupe
  - 12 cashews
  - 2 Tbsp goji berries

(Top with water to MAX LINE & extract)

## VII. Power Booster
- 50% Swiss Chard
- 50 % mixture of fruit:
  - 1/2 banana
  - 1 cup raspberries
  - 10 almonds
  - 1 Tbsp cacao powder

(Top with water to MAX LINE & extract)

## VIII. Swiss Mix
- 50% Swiss Chard
- 50 % mixture of fruit:
  - 1/2 banana
  - 1 cup raspberries
  - 10 almonds
  - 1 Tbsp cacao powder

(Top with water to MAX LINE & extract)

## IX. Free Radical Fighter
- 50% Swiss Chard
- 50 % mixture of fruit:
  - 1 avocado
  - 1 small fig
  - 1/2 cup blackberries
  - 1/2 cup raspberries
  - 10 walnut halves
  - 1 Tbsp chia seeds
  - 1 Tbsp cacao

(Top with water to MAX LINE & extract)

## OR Mix and Match
the following ingredients for your
personalized blast:

### Greens
Fill 50 % of your cup with:
- Kale
- Swiss Chard
- Collard Greens

### Fruits and Vegetables
Fill 50% of your cup with:
- blueberries, blackberries, raspberries, strawberries, grapes (with seeds), melon
- apple, banana, peach, plum, pear, avocado
- small fig, apricot, or nectarine

### BOOSTS
Top off your cup with the following amounts of these ingredients; include one serving of nuts in every stage 3 Blast

- 10 walnut halves
- 12 cashews
- 10 almonds
- 3 Brazil Nuts
- 1 Tbsp goji berries
- 1 Tbsp pumpkin seeds
- 1 Tbsp chia seeds
- 1 Tbsp flax seed
- 1 Tbsp cacao
- 1 Tbsp sesame seed
- 1 tsp maca powder

# ON TRACK SNACKS

## ❶ Veggie Snacks

### A. LifeBoost Dips and Veggies
Serve two of the vegetable servings listed below with two tablespoons of the dips listed below.

### Veggies
- baby carrots or large carrots, peeled and sliced
- celery spears
- bell pepper, sliced
- cucumber, sliced
- cherry tomatoes
- cup sugar snap peas

### LifeBoost Dips
### Hummus (2 Tbsp/serving)
- 2 cloves of garlic
- 2 cups canned chick peas, rinsed and well drained
- 1 tsp sea salt
- 1/3 cup tahini
- Juice of 2 fresh lemons
- 1 Tbsp extra virgin olive oil

#### Preparation:
❶ Place all ingredients in Nutribullet. Pulse with the Extractor Blade several times until well combined but still coarse. Adjust seasonings.

❷ Transfer to serving bowl and serve or cover with plastic wrap.

## LifeBoost Dips
## Classic Guacamole (2 Tbsp/serving)
- 1 ripe avocado, peeled and pitted
- juice of 1 lime wedge
- 1 Tbsp cilantro
- 1/4 cup chopped red onion
- 1/2 clove garlic
- sea salt and pepper to taste

**Preparation:**

**1** Place all ingredients in Nutribullet. Pulse with the Extractor Blade several times until well combined but still coarse.

## Baba Ganoush (2 Tbsp/serving)
- 1/2 large eggplant
- 1 Tbsp tahini
- 1 Tbsp lemon juice
- 1 cloves garlic
- pinch of chili powder
- 1 Tbsp olive oil
- salt to taste

**Preparation:**

**1** Preheat oven to 400

**2** Slice eggplant in half lengthwise and brush with olive oil. Place on foil lined sheet and bake for 45 mins until soft.

**3** Allow eggplant to cool, then scoop out insides and combine in Nutribullet using Extractor Blade with tahini, lemon juice, garlic, and chili powder, discarding the skins.

**4** Drizzle with olive oil and blend again.

**5** Add salt to taste.

## Onion, Spinach, and Artichoke Dip (2 Tbsp/serving)

- 1/2 medium onion
- 1 clove garlic
- 3/4 cup fresh spinach
- 2/3 canned artichoke hearts, drained
- 1 cup nonfat plain Greek yogurt
- 1/2 Tbsp chives
- Fresh cracked pepper to taste
- Sea salt to taste

**Preparation:**

**1** Heat olive oil in a nonstick pan for one minute. Add onions and sauté until caramelized, about 5 to 10 minutes. Add garlic and sauté for 1 minute. Add spinach and cook for two minutes until just wilted. Allow to cool for 5 minutes.

**2** Place spinach-onion mixture and artichoke hearts in the Nutribullet. Pulse with extractor blade 1-3 times until minced. Add yogurt, chives, salt, and pepper. Pulse another 2 to 3 to times until vegetables and dairy are fully mixed.

**3** Serve room temperature or chill in the refrigerator until eating.

## B. Edamame

Enjoy 1 ½ cups of organic, non-gmo (non genetically modified) edamame in the pod or ¾ cups unshelled.

# ON TRACK SNACKS

## ❷ Nutty Snacks

These snacks are tasty, satisfying and very portable. Enjoy!

### A. Nutribars

One bar = one snack

### Nut and Seed Bars

Making your own raw nut and seed bars is a really easy way to make delicious snacks that are perfect to take on the go.

Choose one of the following combinations, or mix and match to create your own:
• Cashew Apricot
• Walnut Date
• Almond Fig
• Pecan Prune
• Sesame Seed Apricot
• Pumpkin Seed Date

**Preparation:**

❶ Fill the Short Cup up to the max line with your favorite nuts.

❷ Use the pulsing technique to grind the nuts into a small, but still chunky consistency.

❸ Add in one fruit of your choice –
  • Apricot – cut off the tip and squeeze out the sticky center of 6 dried apricots into your pulsed nuts.
  • Date – cut off the tip and remove the pit, then squeeze out the sticky center or 4-6 dates into your pulsed nuts.
  • Figs – scoop out the meat of 2-3 ripe figs into your pulsed nuts.
  • Prune - cut off the tip and squeeze out the sticky center of 4 prunes into your pulsed nuts.

❹ Mix the ingredients together in the Short Cup with a spoon.

❺ Take handfuls of the mixture out of the cup and form into rectangular "bars".

❻ Wrap individual bars in wax paper or plastic wrap.

**\*\*Note** – sometimes it's easier to refine the "bar" shape shape once the mixture is in wax paper or plastic. Use the counter top to flatten all four sides and ends.

## Almond Cacao Goji Bar

- Almonds
- Figs
- Cacao Nibs
- Goji Berries
- Cacao Powder

**Preparation:**

**1** Fill the Short Cup up to the max line with almonds. Use the pulsing technique to grind the nuts into small, pieces with a chunky consistency.

**2** Place almond pieces in bowl.

**3** Scoop out the meat of three ripe figs and add to a bowl.

**4** Add in cacao nibs (about 1/4 cup).

**5** Add in goji berries (about 1/4 cup).

**6** Add in 1 Tbsp of raw cacao powder.

**7** Take handfuls of the mixture out of the cup and form into rectangular "bars."

**8** Wrap individual bars in wax paper or plastic wrap.

**\*\*Note** – As with the Nut and Seed Bars, sometimes it's easier to refine the "bar" shape once the mixture is already in wax paper or plastic. Use the counter top to flatten all four sides and ends.

## B. Trail Mix

Make your own energy mix with 14 cashews, almonds, pistachios, or walnut halves and 1 Tbsp unsweetened dried fruit.

## C. Produce N' Nut Butter

Enjoy celery or carrot sticks, pear, apple, or banana with 1 tablespoon of cashew, almond, walnut, or pecan butter.

# SUPER SOUPS

## Enjoy for lunch at any stage.

### Tomato Watermelon Gazpacho

- ¼ small seedless red watermelon (peeled cut into chunks)
- 2-3 large red beefsteak tomatoes (cut into chunks)
- 1 organic cucumber (cut into chunks)
- ¼ bunch parsley (cleaned and roughly chopped)
- ¼ bunch cilantro (cleaned and roughly chopped)
- ½ jalapeno (seeded and cut into chunks)
- ½ qt. tomato juice
- 4 shakes hot sauce
- 1 ½ Tbsp Sherry vinegar
- Lime juice from ½ lime
- ½ tsp. Dijon mustard
- ½ diced avocado (optional)
- Salt and freshly ground pepper

**Preparation:**
Combine all the cut ingredients in a large glass bowl. Pour all the liquids over, and season with the salt and pepper. Allow mixture to marinate for at least a couple of hours, then add to NutriBullet Tall Cup and pulse with Extractor Blade until desired consistency is reached. Chill well before serving. Top with diced avocado if desired.

## Pumpkin Soup

- 1 Tbsp olive oil
- 2 cups chopped onions
- 2 tsp whole wheat four
- 4 cups nonfat, reduced sodium vegetable stock
- 3 cups plain pumpkin purée
- ½ tsp minced garlic
- ½ can black beans
- ½ tsp ground cumin
- ¼ tsp salt
- ¼ tsp ground white pepper
- Dusting of grated nutmeg

**Preparation:**

**1** Caramelize onion in olive oil in a skillet over medium heat.

**2** Sprinkle in the flour and cook, stirring, 2 minutes or until mixture is slightly thickened. Add broth, whisking, then pumpkin, garlic, cumin, salt, and pepper. Bring the soup to a simmer, whisking occasionally and cook 15 minutes, stirring occasionally to prevent scorching. Add beans and cook 15 minutes, stirring occasionally to prevent scorching.

# SUPER SOUPS

### Ginger Pea & Brown Rice Soup
- 2 cups frozen peas (do not thaw)
- 1 1/2 cups low-sodium vegetable stock
- 1 Tbsp green onions
- 1 tsp miso paste
- 1 1/2 tsp ginger, coarsely chopped
- 10 basil leaves, coarsely chopped
- 1/2 cup cooked brown rice

**Preparation:**

**1** Heat peas in stock in a saucepan over medium heat. Cover and bring to a boil, about 10 minutes.

**2** Add all other ingredients except rice. Heat for one minute, then remove pot from heat.

**3** Allow to completely cool, then carefully pour mixture into Nutribullet.* Pulse with Extractor Blade until smooth. Re-heat as needed and pour over cooked brown rice in a bowl.

**\*NEVER BLEND WARM/HOT LIQUIDS IN THE NUTRIBULLET CUPS AS THIS MAY DAMAGE THE PIECES. ALWAYS BLEND COLD OR ROOM TEMPERATURE INGREDIENTS.**

### Tomato Soup
- 4 cups or 2 cans organic plum tomatoes
- 1 cup water or vegetable broth
- 1 onion
- 5 cloves garlic
- 2 medium sweet potatoes, peeled and chopped
- 1 to 2 handfuls of cashews
- salt and pepper to taste

**Preparation:**

**1** Place tomatoes and water/broth in a pot and bring to a boil, adding onion, sweet potato and garlic as they heat.

**2** Once the mixture boils, reduce heat to simmer for 10-15 minutes until potatoes are cooked through.

**3** Remove mixture from heat and allow to cool for 10-15 minutes. Add cooked mixture and cashews to NutriBullet and puree with Extractor Blade until smooth.

## Butternut Squash Soup

- 1 Tbsp olive oil
- 1 cup chopped white or yellow onion
- 1 medium apple, peeled, cored, seeded, and cut into chunks
- 2 ½ lbs butternut squash, peeled, seeded, and cut into chunks
- 4 cups vegetable broth
- 1 Tbsp curry powder
- 1 cinnamon stick or a pinch of ground cinnamon
- ¾ cup unsweetened coconut milk (optional)
- salt
- freshly ground pepper

**Preparation:**

**1** Cook onion, garlic, and apple in a pot in olive oil over medium heat until browned.

**2** Add all ingredients except coconut milk, salt, and pepper. Cover the pot and simmer mixture for 20 to 25 minutes until squash is tender.

**3** Remove from heat, discard cinnamon stick, and cool for at least 30 minutes until cool enough to blend.

**4** Add batches of squash mixture to Nutribullet and puree with extractor blade until smooth.

**5** When ready to serve, return blended soup to pot, add coconut milk, and heat until hot. Add salt and pepper to taste.

# SUPER SOUPS

## White Bean and Veggie Soup (makes 6 servings)

- 1/2 Tbsp olive oil
- vegetable stock
- 1 cup sliced portabella or button mushrooms
- 2 carrots, diced
- 1 large onion, diced
- 2 celery stalks, diced
- 1 summer squash or zucchini, diced
- 4 garlic cloves, minced
- 1 Tbsp fresh basil
- 1 tsp dried thyme
- pinch cayenne pepper
- 1 bunch chopped kale, collards, or chard (stems removed and saved for NutriBlast)
- 2 cups diced tomatoes
- 1 carton vegetable broth
- 2 cups canned white beans (cannellini, great northern, or navy)
- salt and ground pepper to taste

**Preparation:**

❶ Heat oil in a large pot over medium heat. Add mushrooms, onion, carrots, celery, and squash. Cook, stirring often, for 5 to 6 minutes. If veggies start sticking to the bottom of the pot, pour in just enough vegetable stock to keep them from sticking.

❷ Add garlic, basil, thyme, and cayenne, and cook, stirring often, for 1 minute.

❸ Add kale or chard and cook, stirring often, until the leaves have wilted.

❹ Add tomatoes, broth, and beans, stirring to combine. If mixture seems thick, add 1 cup or so of water.

❺ Bring to a simmer, reduce heat to medium-low, and continue to simmer for 20 minutes, stirring occasionally. Season with salt and pepper.

# WELLNESS WRAPS AND SANDWICHES

## Enjoy these for lunch at any stage.

### Quinoa Asparagus Wrap (makes 2 servings)
- 2 whole wheat tortillas
- 1 cup of cooked quinoa
- 10 steamed asparagus spears
- 1/4 cup diced tomato
- 1 handful of alfalfa or sunflower sprouts
- 1 lemon
- 1 Tbsp Veganaise (or garlic aioli)
- Pepper

**Preparation:**

**1** Once cooked per quinoa's instructions, add veganaise and juice of one lemon to one cup of cooked quinoa.

**2** Lay out tortillas on a flat surface.

**3** Divide and spread quinoa mixture onto the tortillas.

**4** Add 5 steamed asparagus spears to each tortilla.

**5** Add diced tomato and sprouts.

**6** Roll up tortillas.

**7** Enjoy.

### Veggie Sandwich
- 2 slices of Low Sodium Ezekiel Sprouted Bread
- Homemade Hummus (pg 87)
- sliced cucumber
- sliced tomato
- sliced red onion (optional)
- 10 leaves of spinach (or other lettuce)

**Preparation:**

Build a yummy sandwich by layering the veggies on the hummus. Delish!

**\*Note** – replace the hummus with any other LifeBoost dip for a tasty variation.

# WELLNESS WRAPS AND SANDWICHES

### Eggplant Red Pepper Wrap

- 1 Whole Wheat Tortilla
- 2 Tbsp homemade baba ganoush* (pg 82)
- Handful of rinsed arugula
- 1/2 raw red pepper, thinly sliced into strips
- ¼ avocado
- Small segment of red onion, thinly sliced
- 1/4 lemon
- Unhulled sesame seeds
- Pepper

**Preparation:**

**1** Lay out tortilla on a flat surface.

**2** Spread baba ganoush onto the tortilla.

**3** Layer arugula, red pepper, avocado, and onion onto the tortilla.

**4** Squeeze the lemon wedge over the ingredients; remove any seeds that fall.

**5** Season with sesame seeds and pepper.

**6** Roll up tortilla.

**7** Enjoy!

**\*Note** – replace the baba ganoush with any other LifeBoost dip for a tasty variation.

## Green Machine Wrap

- 1 Whole Wheat Tortilla
- 2 Tbsp homemade hummus (pg 81) or baba ganoush (pg 82)
- 1 medium kale or chard leaf
- ½ fresh green Serrano chili pepper, diced into small pieces
- sliced cucumber
- sliced tomato
- shredded carrot
- ¼ avocado
- 1 Tbsp all-natural salsa verde
- Unhulled sesame seeds
- Pepper

**Preparation:**

**1** Lay out tortilla on a flat surface.

**2** Spread hummus, baba ganoush, or green pea guacamole onto the tortilla.

**3** Layer kale/chard, chili pepper, cucumber, tomato, carrot, and avocado onto the tortilla.

**4** Spoon salsa over the ingredients.

**5** Season with sesame seeds and pepper.

**6** Roll up tortilla.

**7** Enjoy.

## Superfood Sushi (makes 1 6 to 8 piece roll)

This is a fun way to enjoy Nori—a nutritious sea vegetable—along with your more common raw veggies. Don't get discouraged if your rolls aren't perfect, the more rolls you make, the better your sushi skills will get. Plus, brown rice, veggies, and seaweed taste great no matter what shape they're in!

- 1/4 carrot, shredded
- 1/2 cup spinach or mixed greens
- 1/2 avocado, sliced into lengthwise strips
- 1/4 cucumber, cut into matchstick pieces
- 1/4 carrot shredded or cut into matchsticks
- 2/3 cup sticky brown rice (technique follows)
- 1/4 cup alfalfa or sunflower sprouts
- 1 large sheet of Nori seaweed
- raw, unhulled sesame seeds
- sliced ginger and/or wasabi to garnish
- 1/4 cup Bragg's liquid aminos

### Preparation:

**1** Cook 3 cups of brown rice according to rice instructions, but add an extra cup of water to ensure sushi-worthy stickiness.

**2** Lay out Nori on a hard, flat surface.

**3** Spread ¾ cup (or less) of your prepared sticky rice on the sheet in a thin layer, leaving at least ¼ inch of rice-free Nori borders.

**4** Line strips of veggies at the very edge of the Nori, making sure they do not take up more than ¼ of the entire Nori sheet.

**5** Tightly roll your sushi, but not so tight as to break the Nori.

**6** Seal the edge of the roll by dipping your finger in water and running it across the open edge of the Nori.

**7** Slice roll with a sharp knife into 6 to 8 pieces.

**8** Serve with ginger and/or wasabi, and freely dip your sushi into Bragg's Liquid Aminos, a healthy soy sauce alternative.

# GOOD GRAIN SIDE DISH

## Enjoy for lunch at any stage.

### Wild Rice Lentil and Arugula Salad

- 2 cups cooked wild rice
- 2 cups cooked lentils
- 1/4 cup olive oil
- 1-2 cloves of garlic
- fresh thyme (optional)
- 2 lemons
- 2 cups organic arugula
- 2 tomatoes
- fresh sage (optional)

**Preparation:**

1. Prepare and cool 2 cups of your favorite wild rice blend.
2. Prepare and cool 2 cups of your favorite lentils.
3. Combine rice and lentils in a bowl.
4. Extract 1/4 cup of olive oil, juice of 2 lemons, 1-2 cloves of garlic and fresh sage in the Short Cup until the ingredients are will blended.
5. Pour mixture over the rice and lentils.
6. Toss in 2 cups of fresh arugula.
7. Toss in 1 cup of chopped tomato.
8. Serve chilled or warm. If warm, serve rice and lentils on top of the arugula and pour "dressing" over top.

## Quinoa "Stuffing"

- 2 cups cooked quinoa
- 3 stalks celery
- 2 carrots
- pinch of sea salt
- dried cranberries

**Preparation:**

1. Prepare 2 cups of your favorite quinoa and add to a bowl while still warm.
2. Chop 3 stalks of celery and add to bowl.
3. Chop 2 raw carrots and add to bowl.
4. Add ¼ cup (or more to taste) of dried cranberries and add to bowl.
5. Sprinkle with Himalayan sea salt and serve.

**Alternative:** To create more of a wintertime comfort food – add all ingredients to a casserole dish and bake at 350 for about 25 minutes.

## Quinoa Tabouli

- 2 cups cooked quinoa
- 1/2 medium onion, minced
- 2 cloves garlic, press or chopped
- 2 cups fresh parsley
- 1 medium tomato, chopped
- 3 Tbsp extra virgin olive oil
- 1 Tbsp fresh lemon juice
- sea salt and pepper to taste

**Preparation:**

1. Add 2 cups of cooked quinoa to a bowl.
2. Place onion, garlic, parsley and tomato into the Short Cup and pulse until all of the ingredients are chopped/minced.
3. Pour this mixture over the quinoa.
4. Add olive oil, lemon juice and salt and pepper to the other ingredients and toss together.
5. Refrigerate for 1 hour prior to serving.

## Veggie Potato Salad

- 24 small red potatoes
- 2 ears of sweet corn
- 3 stalks celery
- 2 carrots
- 1 yellow pepper
- 1/4 cup of olive oil
- 1/4 cup of balsamic vinegar
- 1-2 cloves of garlic
- 2 sprigs of fresh thyme

**Preparation:**

**1** Steam 24 small red potatoes and 2 ears of corn until soft.

**2** Chill corn and cut kernels right off of the cobb into the bowl.

**3** Chill and quarter the potatoes and place in bowl.

**4** Chop 3 stalks of celery and add to bowl.

**5** Chop 2 raw carrots and add to bowl.

**6** Chop one yellow pepper and add to bowl.

**7** In Short Cup combine ¼ cup of olive oil ¼ cup of balsamic vinegar, 1-2 cloves of garlic and 2 sprigs of fresh thyme. Blend until smooth.

**8** Pour the mixture over the ingredients in the bowl and toss together.

**9** Chill.

## Mexican Casserole

- 2 cups brown rice
- 1 can organic black beans
- 1 clove of garlic (optional)
- 10 cherry tomatoes
- 1/4 of a small onion
- 4 sprigs of cilantro
- 1 jalapeño pepper
- 1/4 avocado

**Preparation:**

**1** Prepare 2 cups of brown rice.

**2** Heat 1 can of organic black beans with one minced garlic clove on the stove top.

**3** Add 10 cherry tomatoes, ¼ of a small onion, 4 sprigs of cilantro, a jalapeno pepper (optional), and the juice of one lime to the Short Cup and pulse to make salsa.

**4** In a casserole dish, spoon a layer brown rice on the bottom, then beans, then salsa.

**5** Top with sliced avocado (or with a layer of guacamole see page 82).

**6** Serve.

**Note** – Avocado and guacamole turn brown very quickly when exposed to air. Add to casserole just before serving and squeeze lime on top to preserve their green color.

# Chick Pea Summer Salad

While the chickpea is not a grain, it is a complex starch—which is what we want to incorporate in this list. Enjoy this deliciously beany recipe as you would any other Good Grain Side Dish!

- 1 can organic chick peas
- 2 full sized tomatoes (or 20 cherry tomatoes)
- 5 stalks of celery
- 1/4 cup olive oil
- 1-2 cloves of garlic
- fresh thyme (optional)
- 2 lemons

**Preparation:**

1. Chop 5 stalks of celery add to bowl.
2. Chop 2 tomatoes (or quarter about 20 cherry tomatoes) add to bowl.
3. Drain one can of organic garbanzo beans and add to bowl.
4. Extract ¼ cup of olive oil, juice of 2 lemons, 1-2 cloves of garlic and fresh thyme in the Short Cup until the ingredients are well blended.
5. Pour the mixture over the ingredients in the bowl.
6. Sprinkle with Himalayan sea salt.
7. Serve or chill in refrigerator.

**\*Note** – Other favorite veggies, like raw red pepper or artichoke, make delicious additions to this dish.

# GOOD GRAIN SIDE DISHES

## Chard and Pine Nut Risotto

This dish takes some time (and a couple of pots and pans) to prepare, but its decadent flavor and nutritious goodness are well worth the time and effort!

- 1 quart vegetable broth
- 5 cups water
- 1/4 cup pine nuts
- 2 tablespoons olive oil
- 1 cup finely chopped onion
- 2 cloves garlic, finely chopped
- 2 cups uncooked short-grain brown rice
- 4 cups coarsely chopped swiss chard leaves (about 1 bunch)
- Salt and pepper to taste

**Preparation:**

**1** Mix broth and water together and simmer in a large pot. Leave simmering and cover.

**2** Toast pine nuts in a dry skillet over medium-low heat, shaking frequently to brown evenly. Remove from heat when fragrant and brown. Transfer to a separate plate to cool.

**3** Heat oil in a medium pot over medium heat. Add onion and garlic and cook, stirring occasionally, until softened, 4 to 5 minutes. Add uncooked rice and chard and stir gently, until rice is toasted and fragrant, and chard is wilted (roughly 4 to 5 minutes).

**4** Add 1 cup of the broth-water mixture and cook, stirring constantly and adjusting heat if needed to maintain a simmer, until liquid is almost absorbed. Repeat process, adding about 1/2 cup of the broth-water mixture each time until rice is tender, about 35 minutes.

**5** Season to taste, transfer to a medium bowl, and sprinkle with toasted pine nuts.

**6** Enjoy!

# Sweet Potato Oven Cakes (makes 4 servings)

Enjoy this baked version of the pan-fried potato pancake.

- 3 medium sweet potatoes, peeled and coarsely grated
- 1/2 onion
- 1/2 cup 100% applesauce (no sweeteners, thickeners, etc)
- 4 Tbsp whole wheat flour
- 1 tsp baking powder
- 1/2 tsp kosher salt
- 1/4 tsp black pepper

**Preparation:**

1. Preheat oven to 400 degrees.
2. Lightly grease a cookie sheet with olive or coconut oil.
3. Grate potatoes and onion into a large bowl. Add applesauce, flour, baking powder, salt, and pepper and mix thoroughly by hand.
4. Place rounded mounds of the mixture on cookie sheet (about 3" diameter).
5. Bake for 20 minutes, flip with a spatula, and bake on the other side for another 20 minutes or until golden brown.
6. Serve with more applesauce and grated horseradish.

# (MOSTLY) RAWLICIOUS SIDE SALADS

## Cucumber Salad

- 2 hot house or 4 regular cucumbers
- 1 small red onion
- 1/2 cup of Bragg's Apple Cider Vinegar
- 2 pinches of stevia
- 2 sprigs of thyme (optional)

**Preparation:**

**1** Slice 2 organic hot house or 4 regular cucumbers (about ¼ inch thick) and add to a bowl.

**2** Thinly slice a red onion and add to bowl.

**3** Add apple cider vinegar, garlic, fresh thyme (optional) and stevia to the short cup and blend to smooth consistency.

**4** Pour vinegar mixture over the ingredients in the bowl.

**5** Toss and let sit overnight (it's good right away, but it tastes even better when the ingredients hang out together for awhile). Always toss a bit before serving.

## Snappy Succotash (makes 4 servings)

- 1/2 cup cooked edamame
- 1 cup raw chopped green beans
- 1 cup raw chopped cauliflower
- 1 cup raw chopped tomato
- 1 cup raw chopped red pepper
- 4 Tbsp olive oil
- juice of 2 lemons
- 4 Tbsp balsamic vinegar
- 1-2 cloves of garlic
- 2 sprigs of fresh thyme (optional)

**Preparation:**

**1** Put all chopped vegetables into a large salad bowl.

**2** Extract olive oil, lemon juice, garlic, balsamic vinegar and fresh thyme in the Short Cup until the ingredients are will blended.

**3** Pour the dressing mixture onto the veggies and toss together.

**4** Serve or chill.

# (MOSTLY) RAWLICIOUS SIDE SALADS

## Raw Slaw

- 1 cup shredded and chopped carrots
- 1 cup shredded and chopped red cabbage
- 2 cups shredded and chopped green cabbage
- 1 tsp celery seed
- 1 tsp garlic powder
- 2-3 Tbsp fresh pepper
- 2 Tbsp maple syrup
- 3 heaping Tbsp Veganaise
- 1/4 cup lemon juice to taste

**Preparation:**

**❶** Place first 6 ingredients in a large salad bowl.

**❷** Add maple syrup or agave, Veganaise and lemon to the Short Cup. Blend until all of the ingredients are combined well.

**❸** Pour the mixture over the salad ingredients and toss together.

**❹** Chill.

## Veggie Cobb

- 6 cups freshly chopped romaine lettuce
- 1 cup mandarin orange slices (if canned, NO SYRUP)
- 1/3 cup sliced black olives (optional)
- 1/2 cup chopped sweet onion
- 1 avocado, chopped
- 1 cup cherry tomatoes, halved
- ½ cup chilled kidney beans, drained
- 1 cup hearts of palm (diced)
- ¼ cup of olive oil
- juice of 2 lemons
- 1/8 cup of balsamic vinegar
- 1-2 cloves of garlic
- 2 sprigs of fresh basil (optional)

**Preparation:**

1. Place the first 8 ingredients into a large salad bowl.
2. Add olive oil, lemon, balsamic vinegar, garlic and basil to the Short Cup and blend until smooth.
3. Pour dressing over the salad.
4. Devour!!

# (MOSTLY) RAWLICIOUS SIDE SALADS

## Tomacavo-Basil Layered Salad

**Salad:**
- 1/2 beefsteak tomato
- 1/2 avocado
- 8-12 large fresh basil leaves

**Dressing:**
- 1 Tbsp hummus (pg 81)
- 2 Tbsp balsamic vinegar

**Preparation:**
1. Slice tomato into ¼-inch thick slices.
2. Slice avocado into ¼-inch thick slices.
3. Tear off, rinse and dry basil.
4. Layer tomato, basil, and avocado to make a striped presentation.
5. Add hummus and vinegar to the Short Cup and extract until smooth.
6. Pour over salad just before serving.

**Preparation:**
- Serve the salad over a bed of fresh arugula for extra greens.
- Substitute cilantro for basil and red wine vinegar for balsamic for a different flavor combination.

## Sprout and About (serves 4)

- 1 shallot, peeled and thinly sliced
- 1 small fennel bulb, thinly sliced
- 1 1/2 tsp raw agave nectar, or raw honey
- 4 Tbsp apple cider vinegar
- 1 tsp ground mustard seed
- 3 Tbsp olive oil
- Salt and pepper to taste
- 1 pint of cherry or grape tomatoes, halved
- 2 cups lentil sprouts
- 2 cups alfalfa sprouts
- 3/4 pound baby spinach or mâche

**Preparation:**

1. Soak shallot in ice water for 30 minutes.
2. Add vinegar, ground mustard, agave, and olive oil to Short Cup and extract until smooth.
3. Dry shallot and toss with tomatoes, fennel, sprouts, and spinach/mâche.
4. Pour dressing over, toss, and top with salt and fresh ground pepper.
5. Enjoy!

# DINNERS

## Pick one from category A or B and serve with category C.

| A: | or | B: | with | C: |
|---|---|---|---|---|

**A:**

**(4 oz Protein)**

- **Poultry:** chicken breast, turkey breast

- **Seafood:** salmon, halibut, tilapia, trout

- **Red Meat:** Lean beef including round roast/tip, sirloin, and lean ground

**B:**

- 1.5 cups Vibrant Veggie Dinner of your choice (pg 109)

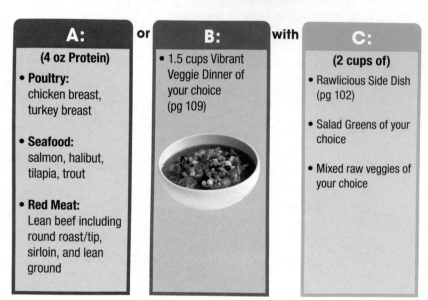

**C:**

**(2 cups of)**

- Rawlicious Side Dish (pg 102)

- Salad Greens of your choice

- Mixed raw veggies of your choice

## ❶ Protein Dinners

Enjoy four ounces of lean protein with 2 cups of the Rawlicious Salad or raw vegetable mixture of your choice.

Meat/fish can be grilled, baked, or pan-seared—no frying or breading. Garnish with fresh lemon juice, balsamic vinegar, Bragg's liquid aminos, or Cobb Salad balsamic vinaigrette (pg 105). Feel free to experiment and create your own sauces – just be sure they follow the plan's guidelines.

# ❷ Vibrant Vegetarian Dinners

**Enjoy 1½ cups of a vibrant veggie dish w/2 cups of the Rawlicious Salad or a raw vegetable mixture of your choice.**

## Lentil Stew

- 2 cups chopped carrots
- 2 cups chopped celery
- 2 cups zucchini
- 1 cup chopped onion
- 1 cup chopped cauliflower
- 1 cup chopped tomato
- 2 cups cooked lentils
- 1/2 - 1 Tbsp extra virgin olive oil
- 4 cups of veggie broth.
- Salt and pepper to taste

**Preparation:**

❶ Add olive oil to the bottom of a large stock pot and heat over medium heat.

❷ Add carrots, celery and onion and sauté until a bit tender.

❸ Add cauliflower and sauté until a bit tender.

❹ Add lentils.

❺ Add veggie broth.

❻ Bring to a boil; then reduce heat back down to low.

❼ Add in tomatoes and heat for 20 minutes.

❽ Salt and pepper to taste.

**Note** – Add your favorite seasonings to taste. Serve with a slice of Ezekiel bread or pour over ½ cup of brown rice, quinoa, or whole wheat pasta.

# DINNERS

## Pasta Fagioli

- 1 cup diced celery
- 1 cup chopped green beans
- 2 carrots, sliced thin
- 2 ripe plum tomatoes peeled & chopped
- 2 Tbsp organic tomato paste, or 1/2 cup tomato sauce
- 1 cup cooked kidney beans or cannellini beans
- 8 oz cooked whole wheat or brown rice pasta
- 1 Tbsp olive oil
- 1 clove garlic, peeled & minced
- 1/2 tsp ground fennel seed
- 1/2 tsp ground coriander seed
- 1 tsp dried basil OR 1 Tbsp
- Salt and pepper to taste
- 2 Tbsp minced fresh basil or Italian parsley for garnish
- 4 cups veggie broth

**Preparation:**

1. Cook pasta according to instructions.
2. Heat the oil on low in a 6 to 8 quart pan.
3. Add the minced garlic to the oil and heat on medium low until lightly browned.
4. Add in carrots, celery, green beans, and chopped fresh tomatoes; sauté 5 minutes on medium high heat.
5. Add the herbs and spices; sauté briefly.
6. Add the veggie broth.
7. Drain and rinse the kidney beans, then add to pot.
8. Add tomato paste or tomato sauce, cover and simmer until veggies are tender.
9. Add the pasta, salt and pepper to taste.
10. Cook for 10 more minutes, adding more water or stock as desired.
11. Serve garnished with fresh basil or Italian parsley.

## Veggie Chili

- 3 cloves of garlic
- 4 tomatoes
- 1 cup chopped carrots
- 1 cup chopped celery
- 1 cup zucchini
- 1 cup chopped onion
- 1 cup chopped bell pepper
- 1 chopped jalapeno pepper (optional)
- 1 can kidney beans
- 1 can pinto beans
- 1 can black beans
- 2 Tbsp oregano
- 1/2 cup veggie broth
- 1/2 Tbsp olive oil

**Preparation:**

1. Place garlic and tomatoes in the Tall Cup and pulse until you've achieved a diced consistency.
2. Add olive oil to the bottom of a large stock pot and heat over medium.
3. Add onion, peppers, carrots, celery and zucchini to the pot and cook until tender.
4. Add extracted tomato mixture, beans, broth and oregano and heat over medium heat while stirring all of the ingredients together for about 10 minutes.
5. Turn heat to low and simmer for about an hour – stirring on occasion.
6. Serve.

# DINNERS

## Butter Bean and Broccolini Soba Noodles

- 1 bundle of 100% whole buckwheat soba noodles
- 1/2 Tbsp coconut or olive oil
- 3-6 stalks of broccolini, depending on size
- pinch of cayenne pepper
- black pepper
- salt
- 10 red or yellow grape tomatoes, halved
- 1/2 cup canned butter beans, rinsed and drained
- 1 Tbsp rice vinegar
- 1 tsp oregano
- 1 tsp basil
- Balsamic or apple cider vinegar, for drizzling

**Preparation:**

1. Bring a large pot of salted water to a boil. Add soba noodles and cook as package directions indicate; then drain and rinse well. Set noodles aside.

2. Steam broccolini until it turns bright green (about two minutes) and set aside.

3. In a nonstick pan, heat olive/coconut oil. Stir in quartered cherry tomatoes, cayenne, salt, and pepper. Add steamed broccolini and let cook for 1-2 minutes so all the pan ingredients get a little caramelized and soften up. Once tomatoes are softened, add butter beans. Stir everything together and pour into a bowl.

4. In the still-hot pan, put 1-2 Tbsp of rice vinegar. Add cooked soba noodles to the vinegar, seasoning with a pinch each of salt, basil, and oregano. Toss to coat the pasta. Once the pasta is coated and heated through, add back the broccolini, beans, and tomatoes. Taste and season with more salt or pepper if needed.

5. Plate, and drizzle with balsamic or cider vinegar if desired.

## Protein Pot

- 1/2 cup uncooked chickpeas
- 1/2 cup uncooked lentils
- 1 cup uncooked speltberries, quinoa, bulgar wheat, or whole wheat pasta
- 1/2 Tbsp olive or coconut oil for sautéing
- 1/2 red onion, chopped
- 3-4 cloves of garlic, minced
- 1 red bell pepper, chopped
- 1 large tomato, chopped
- 3 cups spinach or kale, roughly chopped
- 1/2 cup fresh parsley or cilantro, minced
- 2 Tbsp tahini
- 2 lemon wedges

**Preparation:**

❶ Cook chickpeas and speltberries (or grain of choice) according to package directions. Drain and set aside.

❷ In a large skillet over low-medium heat, add your olive oil and sauté the chopped onion and minced garlic for a few minutes, being careful not to burn. Add the chopped red pepper and tomato and sauté for another 7-8 minutes.

❸ Stir in the chopped kale or spinach and sauté for another few minutes, just until tender. Stir in the tahini, the cooked & drained grains and chickpeas, and simmer on low for another few minutes. Remove from heat and stir in the minced parsley/cilantro. Season with salt and pepper to taste and garnish with lemon wedges and zest. Makes 6 cups.

# DINNERS

## Nut Loaf

- 8 oz chopped mixed nuts
- 1 onion, chopped
- 1 clove of garlic, minced
- 1 red pepper, chopped
- 1/2 cup broccoli, finely chopped
- 1 stick of celery, chopped
- 1 grated carrot
- 1 cup mushrooms, finely chopped
- 2 oz sprouted wheat breadcrumbs** (recipe to follow)
- 1 oz regular, unbleached whole wheat flour
- 5 oz vegetable stock
- 1 tsp thyme
- 1 tsp oregano
- salt and pepper to taste
- 1 Tbsp olive or coconut oil

**Preparation:**

1 Preheat oven to 375 °F.

2 Heat oil in a pan and sauté the onion for a few minutes.

3 Add pepper, celery and mushrooms and sauté for 2 more minutes.

4 Add the garlic and grated carrot and fry for one more minute.

5 Remove from heat; add flour and stir.

6 Add vegetable stock, nuts, breadcrumbs, thyme, oregano, and a little salt and pepper.

7 Grease the inside of a loaf tin with olive oil or olive oil spray. Put the mixture into the tin, pressing it down with a spoon.

8 Bake for around 35 minutes.

9 Slice into ½-thick slices and serve with a large raw vegetable salad.

**\*\*Sprouted wheat breadcrumbs:** Toast two slices of Eziekiel or other sprouted wheat bread to medium brown. Place in Short Cup and pulse 2-3 times in NutriBullet until just broken up.

# Curried Fava Beans (makes 2 servings)

- 1 large yellow onion cut in pieces
- 2 garlic cloves, peeled
- 1-inch piece of fresh gingerroot, peeled and chopped
- 1 Tbsp olive oil
- 1 Tbsp curry powder
- 1/2 tsp ground cardamom
- 1/2 tsp ground cinnamon
- 1/2 tsp dry mustard
- 1/4 tsp cayenne
- 1/4 tsp ground allspice
- 1/4 tsp turmeric
- 1/4 tsp paprika
- 1 cup water
- 1 ½ cups canned fava beans (substitute 1 ¼ c cooked lentils if unavailable)
- 2 medium sized carrots, halved lengthwise and sliced into thin semicircles
- 3/4 cups green peas
- 1/2 tomato, diced
- 3/4 cup light coconut milk
- salt and freshly ground pepper to taste

## Preparation:

1. Pulse the onion, garlic, and ginger in the NutriBullet until smooth.
2. Heat olive oil in a large saucepan over low heat.
3. Add the onion, garlic, and ginger puree, cover, and cook about five minutes to mellow the flavor, stirring occasionally.
4. Stir in the spices, then add carrots and water.
5. Cook, covered, for 20-30 minutes, until carrots are tender.
6. Add the fava beans, tomatoes peas, coconut milk, coconut. Salt and pepper to taste.
7. Simmer another 10 minutes.
8. Serve alone or over ½ cup of brown rice, quinoa, or bulgar wheat.

# DINNERS

## Portabella Burger (makes 4 servings)

- 4 medium portabella mushrooms, stems removed
- 1 medium onion, cut into 1/2 inch slices
- 2 Tbsp olive oil
- 3/4 tsp salt, divided
- 1/2 teaspoon ground black pepper
- 1 avocado, sliced
- 1/2 tsp minced garlic
- 4 whole wheat buns or whole wheat English Muffins, lightly toasted
- 4 jarred roasted red peppers

**Preparation:**

**1** Brush mushrooms and onion slices with oil; sprinkle with 1/2 teaspoon of the salt and 1/4 teaspoon of the pepper.

**2** Heat large skillet or grill pan over medium heat until hot. Add mushrooms; cook until tender, 8 to 10 minutes, turning once. Transfer mushrooms to plate, cavity side up; cover to keep warm.

**3** In same skillet, cook onion slices until golden, about 8 minutes, turning occasionally.

**4** Meanwhile, combine ½ avocado, garlic and remaining 1/4 teaspoon each salt and pepper; mash until smooth. You can also skip this step and use any pre-made guacamole or sweet pea guacamole from the On-Track Snack Dip list (pg 88).

**5** Spoon onions and roasted peppers into mushroom cavities, divided equally. Spread smooth Avocado mixture/guacamole/green pea guacamole on bottom of each bun/English Muffin; top each with stuffed mushrooms.

**6** Top with remaining sliced avocado. Cover with tops of buns/ English Muffins.

**7** Serve with a large raw vegetable salad.

# STAGE ① JOURNAL

| Time | Meal | Ingredients |
|------|------|-------------|
| : | AM NUTRIBLAST | |
| : | AM SNACK | |
| : | LUNCH | |
| : | PM SNACK | |
| : | DINNER | |
| : | EXTRAS | |
| | NOTES COMMENTS/ OBSERVATIONS | |

# STAGE ❶ JOURNAL

| Time | Meal | Ingredients |
|---|---|---|
| : | AM NUTRIBLAST | |
| : | AM SNACK | |
| : | LUNCH | |
| : | PM SNACK | |
| : | DINNER | |
| : | EXTRAS | |
| | NOTES COMMENTS/ OBSERVATIONS | |

| Time | Meal | Ingredients |
|------|------|-------------|
| : | AM NUTRIBLAST | |
| : | AM SNACK | |
| : | LUNCH | |
| : | PM SNACK | |
| : | DINNER | |
| : | EXTRAS | |
| | NOTES COMMENTS/ OBSERVATIONS | |

# STAGE ❶ JOURNAL

| Time | Meal | Ingredients |
|---|---|---|
| : | AM NUTRIBLAST | |
| : | AM SNACK | |
| : | LUNCH | |
| : | PM SNACK | |
| : | DINNER | |
| : | EXTRAS | |
| | NOTES COMMENTS/ OBSERVATIONS | |

| Time | Meal | Ingredients |
|---|---|---|
| : | AM NUTRIBLAST | |
| : | AM SNACK | |
| : | LUNCH | |
| : | PM SNACK | |
| : | DINNER | |
| : | EXTRAS | |
| | NOTES COMMENTS/ OBSERVATIONS | |

# STAGE ❶ JOURNAL

| Time | Meal | Ingredients |
|------|------|-------------|
| : | AM NUTRIBLAST | |
| : | AM SNACK | |
| : | LUNCH | |
| : | PM SNACK | |
| : | DINNER | |
| : | EXTRAS | |
| | NOTES COMMENTS/ OBSERVATIONS | |

| Time | Meal | Ingredients |
|---|---|---|
| : | AM NUTRIBLAST | |
| : | AM SNACK | |
| : | LUNCH | |
| : | PM SNACK | |
| : | DINNER | |
| : | EXTRAS | |
| | NOTES COMMENTS/ OBSERVATIONS | |

# STAGE ❶ JOURNAL

| Time | Meal | Ingredients |
|---|---|---|
| : | AM NUTRIBLAST | |
| : | AM SNACK | |
| : | LUNCH | |
| : | PM SNACK | |
| : | DINNER | |
| : | EXTRAS | |
| | NOTES COMMENTS/ OBSERVATIONS | |

| Time | Meal | Ingredients |
|------|------|-------------|
| : | AM NUTRIBLAST | |
| : | AM SNACK | |
| : | LUNCH | |
| : | PM SNACK | |
| : | DINNER | |
| : | EXTRAS | |
| | NOTES COMMENTS/ OBSERVATIONS | |

# STAGE ① JOURNAL

| Time | Meal | Ingredients |
|------|------|-------------|
| : | AM NUTRIBLAST | |
| : | AM SNACK | |
| : | LUNCH | |
| : | PM SNACK | |
| : | DINNER | |
| : | EXTRAS | |
| | NOTES COMMENTS/ OBSERVATIONS | |

| Time | Meal | Ingredients |
|---|---|---|
| : | AM NUTRIBLAST | |
| : | AM SNACK | |
| : | LUNCH | |
| : | PM SNACK | |
| : | DINNER | |
| : | EXTRAS | |
| | NOTES COMMENTS/ OBSERVATIONS | |

# STAGE ① JOURNAL

| Time | Meal | Ingredients |
|------|------|-------------|
| : | AM NUTRIBLAST | |
| : | AM SNACK | |
| : | LUNCH | |
| : | PM SNACK | |
| : | DINNER | |
| : | EXTRAS | |
| | NOTES COMMENTS/ OBSERVATIONS | |

| Time | Meal | Ingredients |
|---|---|---|
| : | AM NUTRIBLAST | |
| : | AM SNACK | |
| : | LUNCH | |
| : | PM SNACK | |
| : | DINNER | |
| : | EXTRAS | |
| | NOTES COMMENTS/ OBSERVATIONS | |

# STAGE ❶ JOURNAL

| Time | Meal | Ingredients |
|---|---|---|
| : | AM NUTRIBLAST | |
| : | AM SNACK | |
| : | LUNCH | |
| : | PM SNACK | |
| : | DINNER | |
| : | EXTRAS | |
| | NOTES COMMENTS/ OBSERVATIONS | |

# STAGE ② JOURNAL

| Time | Meal | Ingredients |
|---|---|---|
| : | AM NUTRIBLAST | |
| : | AM SNACK | |
| : | LUNCH | |
| : | PM SNACK | |
| : | DINNER | |
| : | EXTRAS | |
| | NOTES COMMENTS/ OBSERVATIONS | |

# STAGE ❷ JOURNAL

| Time | Meal | Ingredients |
|---|---|---|
| : | AM NUTRIBLAST | |
| : | AM SNACK | |
| : | LUNCH | |
| : | PM SNACK | |
| : | DINNER | |
| : | EXTRAS | |
| | NOTES COMMENTS/ OBSERVATIONS | |

www.nutribullet.com

| Time | Meal | Ingredients |
|------|------|-------------|
| : | AM NUTRIBLAST | |
| : | AM SNACK | |
| : | LUNCH | |
| : | PM SNACK | |
| : | DINNER | |
| : | EXTRAS | |
| | NOTES COMMENTS/ OBSERVATIONS | |

# STAGE ② JOURNAL

| Time | Meal | Ingredients |
|---|---|---|
| : | AM NUTRIBLAST | |
| : | AM SNACK | |
| : | LUNCH | |
| : | PM SNACK | |
| : | DINNER | |
| : | EXTRAS | |
| | NOTES COMMENTS/ OBSERVATIONS | |

| Time | Meal | Ingredients |
|---|---|---|
| : | AM NUTRIBLAST | |
| : | AM SNACK | |
| : | LUNCH | |
| : | PM SNACK | |
| : | DINNER | |
| : | EXTRAS | |
| | NOTES COMMENTS/ OBSERVATIONS | |

# STAGE ❷ JOURNAL

| Time | Meal | Ingredients |
|---|---|---|
| : | AM NUTRIBLAST | |
| : | AM SNACK | |
| : | LUNCH | |
| : | PM SNACK | |
| : | DINNER | |
| : | EXTRAS | |
| | NOTES COMMENTS/ OBSERVATIONS | |

| Time | Meal | Ingredients |
|---|---|---|
| : | **AM NUTRIBLAST** | |
| : | **AM SNACK** | |
| : | **LUNCH** | |
| : | **PM SNACK** | |
| : | **DINNER** | |
| : | **EXTRAS** | |
| | **NOTES COMMENTS/ OBSERVATIONS** | |

# STAGE ② JOURNAL

| Time | Meal | Ingredients |
|---|---|---|
| : | AM NUTRIBLAST | |
| : | AM SNACK | |
| : | LUNCH | |
| : | PM SNACK | |
| : | DINNER | |
| : | EXTRAS | |
| | NOTES COMMENTS/ OBSERVATIONS | |

| Time | Meal | Ingredients |
|------|------|-------------|
| : | AM NUTRIBLAST | |
| : | AM SNACK | |
| : | LUNCH | |
| : | PM SNACK | |
| : | DINNER | |
| : | EXTRAS | |
| | NOTES COMMENTS/ OBSERVATIONS | |

# STAGE ❷ JOURNAL

| Time | Meal | Ingredients |
|------|------|-------------|
| : | AM NUTRIBLAST | |
| : | AM SNACK | |
| : | LUNCH | |
| : | PM SNACK | |
| : | DINNER | |
| : | EXTRAS | |
| | NOTES COMMENTS/ OBSERVATIONS | |

| Time | Meal | Ingredients |
|------|------|-------------|
| : | AM NUTRIBLAST | |
| : | AM SNACK | |
| : | LUNCH | |
| : | PM SNACK | |
| . | DINNER | |
| : | EXTRAS | |
| | NOTES COMMENTS/ OBSERVATIONS | |

# STAGE ❷ JOURNAL

| Time | Meal | Ingredients |
|------|------|-------------|
| : | AM NUTRIBLAST | |
| : | AM SNACK | |
| : | LUNCH | |
| : | PM SNACK | |
| : | DINNER | |
| : | EXTRAS | |
| | NOTES COMMENTS/ OBSERVATIONS | |

| Time | Meal | Ingredients |
|---|---|---|
| : | AM NUTRIBLAST | |
| : | AM SNACK | |
| : | LUNCH | |
| : | PM SNACK | |
| : | DINNER | |
| : | EXTRAS | |
| | NOTES COMMENTS/ OBSERVATIONS | |

# STAGE ❷ JOURNAL

| Time | Meal | Ingredients |
|------|------|-------------|
| : | AM NUTRIBLAST | |
| : | AM SNACK | |
| : | LUNCH | |
| : | PM SNACK | |
| : | DINNER | |
| : | EXTRAS | |
| | NOTES COMMENTS/ OBSERVATIONS | |

# STAGE ❸ JOURNAL

| Time | Meal | Ingredients |
|------|------|-------------|
| : | AM NUTRIBLAST | |
| : | AM SNACK | |
| : | LUNCH | |
| : | PM SNACK | |
| : | DINNER | |
| : | EXTRAS | |
| | NOTES COMMENTS/ OBSERVATIONS | |

# STAGE ❸ JOURNAL

| Time | Meal | Ingredients |
|---|---|---|
| : | AM NUTRIBLAST | |
| : | AM SNACK | |
| : | LUNCH | |
| : | PM SNACK | |
| : | DINNER | |
| : | EXTRAS | |
| | NOTES COMMENTS/ OBSERVATIONS | |

| Time | Meal | Ingredients |
|---|---|---|
| : | **AM NUTRIBLAST** | |
| : | **AM SNACK** | |
| : | **LUNCH** | |
| : | **PM SNACK** | |
| : | **DINNER** | |
| : | **EXTRAS** | |
| | **NOTES COMMENTS/ OBSERVATIONS** | |

# STAGE ❸ JOURNAL

| Time | Meal | Ingredients |
|---|---|---|
| : | AM NUTRIBLAST | |
| : | AM SNACK | |
| : | LUNCH | |
| : | PM SNACK | |
| : | DINNER | |
| : | EXTRAS | |
| | NOTES COMMENTS/ OBSERVATIONS | |

| Time | Meal | Ingredients |
|---|---|---|
| : | AM NUTRIBLAST | |
| : | AM SNACK | |
| : | LUNCH | |
| : | PM SNACK | |
| : | DINNER | |
| : | EXTRAS | |
| | NOTES COMMENTS/ OBSERVATIONS | |

# STAGE ❸ JOURNAL

| Time | Meal | Ingredients |
|------|------|-------------|
| : | AM NUTRIBLAST | |
| : | AM SNACK | |
| : | LUNCH | |
| : | PM SNACK | |
| : | DINNER | |
| : | EXTRAS | |
| | NOTES COMMENTS/ OBSERVATIONS | |

www.nutribullet.com

| Time | Meal | Ingredients |
|------|------|-------------|
| : | AM NUTRIBLAST | |
| : | AM SNACK | |
| : | LUNCH | |
| : | PM SNACK | |
| : | DINNER | |
| : | EXTRAS | |
| | NOTES COMMENTS/ OBSERVATIONS | |

# STAGE ❸ JOURNAL

| Time | Meal | Ingredients |
|---|---|---|
| : | AM NUTRIBLAST | |
| : | AM SNACK | |
| : | LUNCH | |
| : | PM SNACK | |
| : | DINNER | |
| : | EXTRAS | |
| | NOTES COMMENTS/ OBSERVATIONS | |

| Time | Meal | Ingredients |
|---|---|---|
| : | AM NUTRIBLAST | |
| : | AM SNACK | |
| : | LUNCH | |
| : | PM SNACK | |
| : | DINNER | |
| : | EXTRAS | |
| | NOTES COMMENTS/ OBSERVATIONS | |

# STAGE ❸ JOURNAL

| Time | Meal | Ingredients |
|---|---|---|
| : | AM NUTRIBLAST | |
| : | AM SNACK | |
| : | LUNCH | |
| : | PM SNACK | |
| : | DINNER | |
| : | EXTRAS | |
| | NOTES COMMENTS/ OBSERVATIONS | |